W9-BLT-960

Lessons in
Letting Go

WITHDRAWN NOV - 2011

Brown County Public Library
205 Locust Lane / P.O. Box 8
Nashville, IN 47448
Telephone & TDD (812) 988-2850
FAX (812) 988-8119

BROWN COUNTY PUBLIC LIBRARY

Lessons in Letting Go

Confessions *of a* Hoarder

CORINNE GRANT

ALLEN&UNWIN

First published in 2010

Copyright © Corinne Grant 2010

All rights reserved. No part of this book may be reproduced or transmitted in
any form or by any means, electronic or mechanical, including photocopying,
recording or by any information storage and retrieval system, without prior
permission in writing from the publisher. The Australian *Copyright Act 1968*
(the Act) allows a maximum of one chapter or 10 per cent of this book, whichever
is the greater, to be photocopied by any educational institution for its educational
purposes provided that the educational institution (or body that administers it) has
given a remuneration notice to Copyright Agency Limited (CAL) under the Act.

Allen & Unwin
83 Alexander Street
Crows Nest NSW 2065
Australia
Phone: (61 2) 8425 0100
Fax: (61 2) 9906 2218
Email: info@allenandunwin.com
Web: www.allenandunwin.com

Cataloguing-in-Publication details are available
from the National Library of Australia
www.librariesaustralia.nla.gov.au

ISBN 978 1 74175 342 4

Internal design by Lisa White
Set in 11.5/18 pt Adobe Garamond by Post Pre-press Group, Australia
Printed and bound in Australia by Griffin Press

© Mixed Sources
Product group from well-managed
forests, and other controlled sources
www.fsc.org Cert no. SGS-COC-005088
© 1996 Forest Stewardship Council

The paper in this book is FSC certified.
FSC promotes environmentally responsible,
socially beneficial and economically viable
management of the world's forests.

10 9 8 7 6 5 4 3 2

Dedicated to the memory of Graham Middleton.
Thank you for your belief and encouragement.

Contents

Prologue

'Corinne, what in Christ's name am I holding?'

I turned around. My ex-boyfriend Thomas was holding what appeared to be a bunch of sticks in his hand. Even though we'd broken up ages ago, he'd agreed to help me move house. He looked like he was regretting it now; we'd been packing for hours.

We were both standing in the open-plan living area, surrounded by cardboard boxes, old doonas, stuffed toys and what may or may not have once been a fancy-dress caterpillar costume. The kitchen, just behind Thomas, was littered with plastic bags and bits of packing tape. There were pots and pans sitting on the bench tops and the bits of material I'd strung across the windows in a pathetic attempt at home decoration were sagging. If anyone had walked in at that moment, they would have assumed they were looking at a typical flat in the process of being packed up. They wouldn't have known that my flat looked like this all the time. In fact, right now, with the packing under way and half-filled boxes and bags strewn amongst the usual clutter, it was looking decidedly better than it had done in months.

'Well?' Thomas rattled the bunch of sticks at me.

I attempted a light, carefree laugh. What came out of my mouth sounded more like a chicken being strangled. I took a deep breath.

'They're the first bunch of flowers a boy ever gave me. It was back when I was at university and—'

'They're dead.'

'Nooooo,' I explained. 'They're a *dried arrangement*.'

'They're brown. And dead. They are dead, brown sticks.' He went to throw them in the garbage bag.

'Wait!' I grabbed his arm. 'You don't get to make that decision.'

I'd had enough. We'd been packing most of the night and I had already thrown out a whole lot of things because Thomas had told me to—not because I wanted to—and I was not throwing these out as well. I could feel the panic rising.

He held open the garbage bag and suggested I look inside and tell him what, precisely, I thought I should be taking back out again. The broken bread bin? The coffee cup that no longer had a handle? The ripped, blank Christmas cards we had found, inexplicably, under the fridge? To my shame, I started to cry.

'The sticks are different. Please don't make me throw them out.'

Thomas sighed and rubbed his eyes.

'Corinne, I just can't bring myself to put these in a box. I just can't. This is getting ridiculous.'

I thought about it for a moment. He was right, obviously. I was being foolish. They looked nothing like flowers anymore.

'Okay. We'll throw them out.'

He looked relieved.

'But I want to take a photo of them first.'

Thomas held the flowers at arm's length, refusing to be in the photo with them, and I framed up and clicked the camera. Then we threw them in the bin. I felt better and worse simultaneously. Thomas and I had lived together when we were a couple, but only now did I feel like I was letting him see me naked for the first time. And not naked in a good way but bad naked, like he'd just caught me taking a dump in the shower.

The photo was unnecessary, I can see that. Not only was it unnecessary, it was probably an indication of clinical insanity. And yet, that photo turned out to be what saved everything.

It floated back into my life a few years later, escaping a box that had fallen from the wardrobe. I'd been having a bad day. I'd been trying desperately, for the hundredth time, to pare back my belongings and for the hundredth time it wasn't working. I'd lost my temper, thrown a few things around, yelled a lot and sworn at my stuff. In turn, my stuff had retaliated by hurling itself out of the wardrobe. Not content with that, the boxes of rapidly descending crap had then proceeded to knock over my favourite mirror, which smashed to smithereens at my feet. It was hard not to take the whole thing personally. It was equally hard not to go a little floppy and start sobbing. Of all the things I owned, that mirror meant the most.

As I was standing there—surrounded by broken glass, old magazines, all of my pencils from primary school, two Eiffel Tower–shaped key-rings, a miniature bottle of Malibu, half a stapler and what I was praying was a ball of hair that had once belonged to a doll and not a human—I saw the photo of Thomas and the sticks. I picked it up. I had no idea what I was looking at. It appeared to be a picture of someone's arm holding . . . what? Twigs? Branches? Really ordinary divining rods? Why had I taken a photo of this? Why had I—oh my god. Oh. My. God.

That was the day I realised I was a hoarder and also, if I was honest with myself, perhaps a little unhinged.

It took a year to drag myself out of the mess. A year in which I lost my dearest friend and then promptly lost my way. A year in which I ran away overseas, came back and then ran away again. A year in which I learnt to let go, learnt to forgive, learnt to grow up and learnt that we can all accidentally find ourselves filming dog porn when we thought we were filming something else. It was a big year. It was a lot of work.

But before all of that, before I could even begin to clear out my life, I had to figure out where it all started. Irrespective of how it may look to an outsider, hoarders don't just pop out of the ground fully formed. Hoarding isn't something anyone is aware of until it's too late. Hoarding sneaks up on you in the middle of the night wearing dark glasses and a false moustache and weasels its way in when you're not looking.

Before the stuff went, I was going to have to get to the truth of the matter. And the truth of the matter is this: hoarding doesn't start with the stuff. It starts with something else.

And that something else is much, much harder to get rid of.

Part 1
Where It Started

Chapter One

I was in Albury–Wodonga the first time I experienced regret. I was eight years old. I was standing next to another little girl in Waltons department store, looking down through the railings of the first floor to the toy section below. The other girl was the same height as me and had dark hair and a red pinafore. She turned her head, looked right at me and asked which I liked better, bears or dolls. I was so overcome by terror that instead of answering, I ran away.

The reason I was so terrified in the first place had a lot more to do with Albury–Wodonga than the little girl in the red pinafore. I grew up in Corryong, which was (and still is) one hundred and twenty-four kilometres to the east of Albury–Wodonga. We didn't have department stores, or roundabouts or traffic lights or our very own Darrell Lea. Instead, we had a guy we claimed was the Man From Snowy River buried in our cemetery. We also had two supermarkets, two butchers, two banks and a swimming pool so iridescently blue you needed a welding mask to look at it directly. We had eleven hundred people. We also had two pubs: the Top Pub, which was at the top end of town, and the Bottom Pub, which wasn't. Apart from that, there wasn't much else. It was a beautiful, friendly, perfect town in which to grow up but it wasn't a fancy town. And I was definitely not a fancy kid.

We were Top Pub folk and every Friday night we would go there for what we called 'tea' but city folk probably called 'dinner'. Mum, Dad, my sister Wendy and I would sit in the ladies' lounge in front of the giant TV screen and us kids would watch our favourite programme, *The Dukes of Hazzard*. I loved Bo Duke so hard it made my eyes water.

We knew everyone else in the Top Pub and if we didn't know them by name, we could pick which family they belonged to from their physical traits. That blond guy with the big head sitting near the fernery? Had to be a Smithton. That woman with the low-slung backside and curly hair? Definitely a Framer. That skinny red-headed kid screaming and racing around the condiments table with a fork? That was one of the Tully boys. Run.

Occasionally there would be a family from out of town and all us kids, sitting quietly with our parents, hands folded in our laps or placed carefully on the tops of the faux-wood laminate tables, would watch them out of the corners of our eyes, secretly hoping these strangers might be the drama we were looking for. We were watching to see if they ordered the same food as us and if they didn't it would be the topic of conversation in the playground for days to come. 'They let their kids order from the adult menu! She was my age and she had *a whole Chicken Maryland to herself.*' Everyone would get in on the act and it would become a running joke: 'Hey, Tony, what have you got for lunch? Bet it's not *a whole Chicken Maryland.*' 'What are you drawing, Virginia? Is it *a whole Chicken Maryland*?' 'Burke and Wills would have survived if their parents had given them *a whole Chicken Maryland.*' Strangers were something to be discussed and dissected, like rumours of ghosts, or aliens, or kidnappers leaping straight from the pages of an Enid Blyton book. No wonder I was so overwhelmed by that little girl in Albury–Wodonga; I'd never had contact with people I had not known my whole life.

We went to Albury–Wodonga every couple of months to see dentists or doctors and to buy all the things we couldn't get in our own small town. Albury–Wodonga had fluorescent socks, hyper-colour T-shirts and shops that sold just one thing, like cassette tapes or underwear or ice-cream. In my town, we had a hairdresser that doubled as a trophy engraver and tripled as a gun dealer. (It was probably the only shop in the world where you could get a freshly shot duck not only professionally mounted but permed at the same time.) Albury–Wodonga had streets and streets and floors and floors of novelty and speciality and single-purpose stores. The fact that the townsfolk did not walk their own streets slack-jawed in wonder at the sheer amount on offer was very impressive and very cool. These people were way out of my league. They probably ate Chicken Maryland every night.

We would drive down to Albury–Wodonga in Nanna's '66 Holden Special. My grandmother didn't drive so the car was rarely used and consequently, more than a decade after its purchase, still smelt new. The seats were leather, the little hand straps that hung from the roof in lieu of seatbelts smelt like leather, even the floor smelt like leather. It also had a white venetian blind on the rear windscreen that crinkled with a tinny sound every time I touched it.

Nanna used to pack a little waterproof purse with two wet face washers and it would sit on the sill behind the back seats, warming in the sun for the entire trip. When we got to the city we would use the cloths to wipe down our faces and hands and any detritus we had managed to spill on ourselves during the trip. The face washers were hot and sun-warmed and smelt like the inside of the purse. To this day, the slightly toxic and suffocating smell of hot plastic comforts me.

Halfway through our day trip we would inevitably wind up in Waltons department store for lunch. Waltons had automatic sliding doors that looked like real doors because they were made out of wood, which proved to me that it was definitely a posh shop. It sold everything, from clothes to furniture to appliances and it had a cafeteria on the top level overlooking the floors below. For some peculiar reason they did not have prawn cutlets on their menu, so I always ordered the second most sophisticated meal I could imagine: ham, cheese and pineapple on toast.

On the day that would turn out to be my last without regret, I was on tiptoes at the balustrade, looking straight down. Years later, Waltons would shut down, the toy section would become a nightclub and I would go there and consume vastly injurious quantities of raspberry-flavoured lemonade and vodka, but for now I was eight, looking at toys and wondering if I could convince my mother that we should go down the stairs for a closer look. As I was daydreaming, the little girl in the red pinafore came and stood beside me. Then she spoke to me. I froze. This city girl, this fancy city girl with her shops full of stuff and her traffic lights and cinemas and Daisy's Baked Potatoes was actually standing right there and talking. To. Me.

A big part of me wanted to answer her—I was imagining the thrill of going to school the next day and announcing I had made a new friend *that nobody else knew*—but an even bigger part of me was scared. I had no idea how to speak to someone I had never met. This girl was obviously worldly. One glance at the rakish angle of her scrunchie could have told you that. I twitched nervously. There was probably a protocol to answering her and if I got it wrong, I would make a fool of myself. It was a risk too big to take. So instead of replying I stared at her, gaping mutely. Then I ran away.

Almost immediately, I recognised my mistake. This was my first chance for an adventure and I had blown it. What had I done? I stopped running. I was pretty sure she had asked me if I liked the toys. I would go back and answer yes, yes I did like the toys; in fact, I was quite partial to a Strawberry Shortcake doll, followed closely by a Barbie doll and if forced into a corner, I would accept a Puggle. Yes, that was it, I would simply go back and strike up a conversation like nothing weird had happened, like I had never run away from her with my mouth hanging open and we would end up best friends. But when I returned to the spot where she had been, she had disappeared. Just like that, like she had never been there. She didn't even leave a puff of smoke. It dawned on me that this was the first time in my life that I had met someone I would never see again. The idea that some people existed and then they didn't and you could never go back and fix your mistakes was a new and not entirely pleasant concept.

I spent the rest of the day hoping I would find her. I looked for her in the supermarket, in Lincraft, in Darrell Smailes Audio, in Darrell Lea. I even hoped to see her in the dentist's waiting room and hope was not a feeling I normally had there.

For months after the encounter with the girl in the red pinafore I would wake in the middle of the night with an overwhelming feeling of dread. It was so strong it would make it hard for me to breathe. I was tortured by the belief that I had hurt the girl's feelings and, worse, that this could have been my first big adventure and I had run away from it. It felt like the biggest mistake of my life. It probably was. I was only eight.

Each night I lay in bed and replayed the memory over and over in my head and then, because I couldn't stop myself, I would start imagining what had happened to her after I left. A mutated version of a Hans Christian Andersen favourite would play out behind my eyelids: my little Waltons girl, filled with sorrow and a sense of abandonment, ends up homeless, wearing a tattered shawl and selling matches on a street corner until one freezing New Year's Eve, so cold she can barely breathe, she lights her final match to keep herself warm. Then she dies of hypothermia. Heartbroken, cold and alone, her final vision is of me running away from her.

It did not occur to me until years later that she probably just shrugged it off and went back to looking at the toys. Even if I had hurt her feelings, I am sure her mother would have given her an ice-cream and everything would have been set right. Until that day, ice-cream would have fixed things for me also but now everything was tinged with guilt. I would eat an ice-cream and feel sad for all the starving African babies who would never know what it was like. I desperately needed to redeem myself and there seemed to be only one way to do that: I would finger-knit my school a new volleyball net.

Every lunchtime and recess, after school, before school, during school, I finger-knitted. I would sit, huddled over my own hands, carefully winding the wool around my finger, sliding loops through loops, creating a little chain of woolly deliverance. Whenever anyone asked me what I was doing, I would announce proudly: 'I'm making us a new volleyball net.' I had grand visions of an unveiling involving the town mayor, a plaque and possibly an engraved cup—with or without a freshly shot duck. I also had grand visions of once again getting a full night's sleep, unhaunted by visions of the little girl in Waltons.

Understandably, my mother baulked at my request for enough wool to finger-knit a volleyball net and I was instead pilfering little scraps from art classes and from cupboards at home. I became furtive and obsessed, scrabbling for any bits I could, regardless of length, colour or quality. It was hard, slow work and after a month I had only managed to make a line of knitting that stretched twice across the lounge-room floor. It would have taken five hundred times that amount to make a volleyball net. Miserable, I gave up. Who was I kidding? I wasn't cut out to be a martyr, I didn't have the sticking power. I put the finger-knitting in a cupboard. One day, I would return to it. One day, I would set things right again.

What had started as an attempt to right a wrong had now turned into something far more irrational. I was a child; I believed in fairies and dragons and princesses and witches. I believed in happily-ever-afters and now, after the little girl in Waltons, I'd started to believe that if I threw away my stuff, I'd never be able to fix the things I'd broken. It didn't matter if the stuff in question had nothing to do with the thing I'd damaged or hurt or

12

wrecked in the first place—I simply, magically, believed that if I kept it all I would never have to experience sadness, regret or guilt again.

Everything went into the cupboard after that. Broken dolls, old pencil cases, posters and stamps and stickers still in their packaging. I kept Christmas presents I had barely touched, thinking I would play with them one day and allay the guilt I felt on account of all the poor children who had nothing. I kept a lidless toy teapot because throwing it out would have forced me to accept that I'd lost the lid and it was never coming back. When the cupboard was full, I started on a drawer. I carefully stacked away all my birthday cards, the stubs of pencils, bits of eraser, lone buttons and broken necklaces. When the drawer was filled, I found another and another, and then I used the wardrobe and under my bed and the spare room and then the tops of dressers and drawers and desks. It started when I was eight and it never, ever stopped.

Chapter Two

Still, life was far from dire; I had a best friend. Her name was Katie and she was a free spirit, skipping through life with lopsided pigtails and a crooked grin. I ran panting and sweating along behind her, worried that my dress might get dirty, that my shoes might get ruined or that I might step on an ant and ruin an entire insect community's reason for existing. Katie just laughed and ran. She was fearless in the face of regret. With her red hair, freckles and novelty socks, she was partly my best friend and partly my god.

Katie and her family had moved to our town because of her father's job and although Katie had originally been an outsider, it didn't really count as she'd arrived when we were all too young to realise the importance of her foreignness. I am sure it had been different for her parents. A strict protocol came into play whenever there were new people in our town. First, you sat back, watched and listened. There was no initial contact. Instead, you would ask the shopkeepers what the new person was like, you would check out what they bought in the supermarket, you would talk to their work colleagues, you would find out what church they attended and how often. You would find out whether they were Top Pub or Bottom Pub folk. Eventually, after fifty or sixty years, someone would approach them on the street and call them by their first name.

Katie's father never went to the pub at all. This was unheard of in my world. Until I met Katie, I had no idea there were people like her family, people who had chosen to live their own lives, heedless of the need to fit in. When I first met them, I didn't know whether to be awestruck or to report them to the police. For a start, they were the only people I'd come across who didn't mind unexpected visitors. This was shocking. One of our biggest social rules was that no one dropped in unannounced. You couldn't just knock on someone's back door and yoo-hoo your way into their kitchen. What if they were cleaning the stove? How were you supposed to carry on a civilised conversation with someone when their head was in the oven and you were conversing with their apron-covered arse? The casual drop-in was only acceptable if you were absolute best friends, sisters or, in some circumstances, a spouse. Everyone else rang, arranged it at church, or met on neutral territory, such as a fête or funeral.

In our house, unannounced visitors were our greatest fear. Growing up I assumed we were the only house that had to do last-minute cleaning before visitors arrived. That assumption was based on the fact that every other house I knew was showroom-tidy when we went to visit. It never occurred to me that everyone else might be exactly the same as us, running around the house at ten o'clock the night before, cleaning and shoving things in cupboards and under beds. Country people are house proud. Gleaming silver, polished furniture and starched doilies are part of what makes us who we are; it's a tradition that connects us to each other and to our past. There's nothing wrong with that, but it does make it hard to have company.

None of these rules existed at Katie's house. Not only were unexpected visitors never a problem, cleaning was never a problem either. It didn't matter to them that there were unwashed dishes in the sink, undusted ornaments on the mantelpiece and toys on the front lawn. It was shocking, exotic and somewhat unnerving. Walking into their house was like accidentally seeing them nude.

Katie's house had one sitting room at the front which was relatively tidy and then a bunch of unkempt rooms that were adventures on a Narnia-like scale. They even had a chook shed and an out-of-control passionfruit vine that we picked the fruit from in summer. We were allowed to cook in the kitchen unsupervised. We would boil tins of condensed milk, forgetting about them until they exploded. I don't remember ever getting into trouble. I also don't remember ever cleaning up the mess.

Katie's bedroom was nothing like mine. It was messy like mine, but it was the mess of living. Clothes and well-loved toys and dress-ups littered her room. My room was full of broken and half-finished things, long-forgotten craft projects, domino sets missing half the dominoes and deflated balloons. Whenever my poor, exasperated mother insisted that I clean up, I would listlessly move things around, incapable of making a decision to throw something out. I just kept rearranging things and carefully finding hidey-holes for them in the already full cupboards and wardrobes. I was an eight-year-old curator of crap.

Katie was completely different. She would play with things and then throw them out when their usefulness had passed. I couldn't do that at home. For god's sake, I didn't *want* to do that at home. But at Katie's house I could. The first time I ripped up one of her old skirts to make a curtain for a cubby-house window, I was a goner. I was wound up so tightly that I came undone with the centrifugal force of a small tornado. I spun through Katie's lounge room, slightly breathless and high-pitched. 'Can I touch this?' 'Can we cook this?' 'Can I throw this over the fence and listen to next-door's dog rip it up?' I forgot that I needed redemption. At Katie's house, I discovered I could be temporarily unburdened from my conscience.

With all that freedom, I had no choice but to become a tyrant.

It was in Katie's caravan that I finally pushed things too far. Katie's younger brother had a best friend called Craig and often the four of us would play together. We had sleepovers in the caravan, all curled up in our sleeping bags, pretending we were in the outback or on the run from kidnappers. I loved that caravan so much that sometimes I would sneak out to it on my own. Entering it was like climbing into a magical wardrobe, or up a magical tree—normal rules didn't exist in there. Maybe that's why I chose it as the scene of my crime.

At the age of six, Craig was a slight and gentle boy. Once, yipped up on the freedom of Katie's house, I had chased him around a piano until he collapsed. That's the kind of thing I could do when I was there. In the same way animals flee to safer ground just before a natural disaster, Craig would often disappear whenever I came near. It just made me chase him harder.

Even though he was two years younger than me, I wanted to kiss Craig. Kissing a boy seemed like the most reckless thing I could do. (It still does.) How I was supposed to go about it, however, was a mystery to me. From what I had observed, girls did not do the kissing; we waited until a boy kissed us. That did not appeal to me at all as it left me open to random advances. The white-haired boy who had helped me when my parka zipper got stuck might turn out to be fine boyfriend material, but the boy who wet himself whenever he saw sawdust definitely would not. I couldn't leave these things to chance and besides, Craig didn't seem like he was going to kiss me of his own volition. If I wanted this to happen, I was going to have to do it myself. Like a lame gazelle wandering into lion territory, Craig never stood a chance.

Our first (and last) kiss was in Katie's caravan. I had lured him there with the promise of showing him something. I had not thought through what the 'something' was but I had hoped that as soon as we got into the caravan it would come to me. Craig followed warily. As luck would have it, there was a Rod Stewart cassette near the tape player and I used that as my ruse. As Rod's husky voice crooned out 'Sailing', I swung around, knocked Craig down onto the bed and planted one on his lips. He was too stunned to fight back.

It was not quite as romantic as I had imagined it would be. Mainly because, unbeknownst to me, he was eating a black jellybean and when I kissed him, he choked a little bit and black stuff oozed from his mouth. For one brief, confusing moment, I thought I had struck oil.

After that, I announced to everyone who would listen that Craig and I were boyfriend and girlfriend. Our lips had touched in a caravan and according to my books that meant we were practically married. As often happens with young love, however, our romance didn't last long. In fact, it only lasted until he found out that I was telling everyone he was my boyfriend. In hindsight, I can see that it was never going to work. There was not only the age difference to contend with, but we also wanted different things out of life. I was into My Little Pony, he liked Skeletor, I wanted to grow up to be an aerobics instructor, he wanted to eat Clag. Also, if I had stopped to think about it at the time, I would have realised he was just not ready for a serious, committed relationship. Probably because he was six.

It was an ugly break-up. I didn't know back then that it was best to walk away from these things, to saunter off with your head held high and your dignity intact. I was eight, I lacked subtlety, diplomacy and consideration. I lacked restraint. I called Craig a poo breath. He called me a bag of sick-up. I called him a blood blister. He called me a wart face. I called him a virgin. Being called a virgin should not have caused offence to a six-year-old—in fact, it should have been considered a good thing—but at that age when you don't know what a word means, you assume the worst. I called him a virgin, he cried and that was the last I saw of him. I didn't care, he had spurned me; disappearing was the least he could do. Unlike the little Waltons girl, Craig deserved all he got.

I didn't see him again until many years later, when we were both adults. It was at a birthday party in Melbourne and I recognised him immediately.

He was unmistakably Craig; he looked exactly the same except taller and less frightened. I hesitated, worried that he might not remember me or, worse, that he would. Eventually, curiosity got the better of me and I gulped down a glass of champagne and went over. I tapped him lightly on the shoulder and as he turned he grinned, then immediately reminded me of the time I had accosted him in a caravan. Then he told me he was gay.

Even though I knew it was illogical, a small voice in the back of my head whispered, 'You turned Craig gay.'

As Craig laughingly recounted every gory detail of that caravan assault, I thought back to the little Waltons girl and inwardly marvelled at my idiocy. You spend your life trying to make up for a crime you think you've committed and, in the end, it turns out you're guilty of something else entirely.

Chapter Three

I had moved to Melbourne a few years before my reunion with Craig, leaving my childhood behind, hidden in cupboards, wardrobes and drawers. Coming from such a small country town, it took the entire length of my university degree to settle in and, needless to say, when I first arrived my terror was so intense that I was virtually vibrating. There were more people in my art history class than had been in my entire high school.

I had spent a year in Albury–Wodonga before moving to Melbourne, trying to acclimatise to living away from home. I had loved it. Now that I was almost a grown-up, Albury–Wodonga was the perfect size for a country girl spreading her wings. I had thrived there. I'd made new friends, I'd been invited to parties, I'd even kissed a couple of boys without having to concuss them first or lock them in caravans. But Melbourne was different. Melbourne was unfathomably huge. I regressed instantly.

I spent my first year going straight to class then scurrying back to my dorm, where I would eat ice-cream from the bucket and listen to old-time radio because it reminded me of home. I was too scared to find a new hairdresser, so I let my permed hair grow out until the straight part reached my ears and the bottom half remained curly. (I looked like a cocker spaniel.) I wandered around in a pair of purple leggings and a hand-knitted jumper and I was always surprised when people figured out I was from the country without my even mentioning it. It seemed that I was destined to never fit into the city.

Maybe this was the way it was always going to be, I thought. After all, I'd been in Melbourne on my own once before and things had not gone well that time either.

I had been fifteen and had wangled my way into doing work experience at a city radio station. Luckily, I had a second cousin who lived nearby and I was going to stay with him and his family. It should have been a chance to learn about the world and gain some desperately needed experience about living in it. Instead, I arrived at my cousin's house with only one goal for the entire week: to make sure that no one realised I was from the country.

My biggest problem was my country accent. I often replaced the word 'yes' with a sharp intake of breath. It was a habit I had picked up from my grandmother and her friends. If you agreed with someone and words seemed like too much of an effort, you simply gasped instead. If you strongly agreed, you might gasp twice in rapid succession. To the unaccustomed ear we probably sounded like we were choking. I had nightmares that if anyone in the city heard me doing this, they would point at me and start yelling, 'Cow rooter!' I practised saying 'yeah' and 'cool' and 'yeah, cool' and 'cool, yeah' under my breath for a whole week before I left.

My second problem was wardrobe. (My mother had already refused to buy me a power suit like the ones Melanie Griffith wore in the movies.) I fossicked through my wardrobe and dragged out what I thought was my most cosmopolitan outfit. I started with a pair of grey, stretch-flannel culottes: a pair of pants so wide-legged that when you were standing with your legs together they looked like a skirt. Then, for reasons only my fifteen-year-old brain could possibly justify, I chose to team them with a hand-knitted jumper with a picture of a clown on the front. Looking back on it now, I doubt they even dressed Special Needs kids like that.

I wore this ensemble to my first day of work experience. I was very nervous. I had arrived at my cousin's house the night before and things had got off to a bad start. Wanting to prove what a worthy addition to their household I was going to be, I threw myself headlong into playing with my cousin's seven-year-old daughter. We both played with her dolls, she showed me her sticker collection, we danced to her favourite cassette tape. We were getting along very well until I knocked out her front tooth. I still have a photo of this silken-haired little girl in a ruffled denim skirt and blue top, riding the stuffed horse that moments later I tripped over, sending it and her halfway across the room. Even then she probably would have landed unscathed if her face had not glanced off my elbow. I found the tooth underneath the coffee table, half buried in the shag pile. At least we had something to give the Tooth Fairy.

The next morning, with mercurochrome covering the tooth-shaped divot in my elbow, I was standing at the entrance to a shopping centre the size of my entire town, somewhere in the middle of which was the radio station where I would be working. I set my face in what I hoped looked like a world-weary, urbanite expression and walked through its automatic doors.

City people take it for granted but for country kids, coming to the city for the first time is quite overwhelming. There are all the buildings, the traffic and the people speaking in complete sentences to contend with, not to mention the loose-toothed children. These people working at their fancy easy-listening radio station probably all drove Porsches and spoke in nothing but rapid-fire wisecracks. They probably all had share portfolios and lived in condos. They probably hung out with famous people like Boz Scaggs.

I was going to be spending my week with the station's copywriter. It was the closest thing to show business I thought I could handle. I had not dared to apply for anything to do with actual performing; the idea of real actors and directors flipped my heart right over. I reasoned I would start in the background so that if I made a mess of it, I did not have as far to fall, and if I somehow managed to do all right, I wasn't over-reaching myself. Some people are frightened of failure, others of success. I was frightened of both.

I had my head down, concentrating hard on walking properly in my one-inch heels, so it was not until I was well inside the shopping centre that I noticed the escalator. I faltered. We didn't have escalators in the country. We had stories about escalators though: stories about people getting minced by them. I looked around nervously for an elevator. The radio station was one floor down. Everyone I knew back home was well aware of the fact that if you did not jump off an escalator in time, you would get sucked into the grate at the bottom, go all the way around inside the machine and come back out the top looking like coleslaw. Hundreds of people had been injured on escalators, including, I had heard, a girl who had been scalped. Or something like that. Maybe she just caught her hair a little bit. Either way, it was a close call and not a story whose veracity I wanted to test with my own head.

I was starting to perspire by this time. I stared down at the escalator, desperate. If the clown on my jumper had been able to move, it would now have been doing an impression of Munch's *The Scream*. I had to do this, I thought to myself. Nothing was going to expose me as a country bumpkin more than running away from fancy stair technology. I looked down again and forced myself to walk onto it. It was then I realised the escalator wasn't moving. It was just sitting there, its vicious teenager-chewing teeth motionless. Even I could figure out that a stationary escalator was essentially the same as stairs, and stairs were something I was familiar with. Stairs I could do. My confidence returned. I was going to do this, I was really going to do this! I was going to walk down an escalator like it was something I did every day and then I was going to waltz into my first day of work experience, crack some terribly witty gag about technology and everyone would think I was so cool they'd invite me to a disco.

23

I started walking down, thinking to myself, 'I'm fitting in, look at me fitting in!' I looked up to see if other people were noticing me, heedless of the need to watch where I was going and heedless of the fact that I was wearing what were about to become death-trousers. The culotte is a wide-legged pant, and not an article of clothing made for young women with coordination issues and a slightly scatterbrained approach to walking. As I gaily skipped down the non-moving escalator, the heel of one little shoe got caught in the cuff of the other little trouser leg and I tripped. I managed to grab hold of the handrail, saving myself from smashing headfirst into the steps, but my feet were gone from underneath me. I fell down the rest of the escalator. Or, more correctly, I half slid, half fell as I held onto the railing the whole way, making a loud squeaking noise as the rubber and the skin of my wrist fought a battle to see who could handle friction best. The rubber won.

Not surprisingly I caused quite a scene. As I lay on the shopping centre floor a few feet from the escalator, staring at the ceiling two floors above me, with rubber burns on one wrist and bleeding from one ankle, a security guard ran over. He knelt beside me and asked if I was all right. My stockings were in tatters, my woolly, clowny friend was skewed around my little flat chest and all the fight had gone out of me. Everything I had been working so hard to conceal sprang back to the surface and I uttered the first words that came into my head.

'I'm from the country.'

No one invited me to a disco that night, although they did let me pop out to buy a new pair of stockings to replace the ones shredded by the escalator. They also gave me some Bandaids.

Now, just a few years later and living in Melbourne permanently, the trauma of that incident was still fresh in my mind. Thank god I went to a university that didn't have escalators. And thank god I still had that clown jumper with me. I didn't wear it anymore, of course, but I'd brought it down to Melbourne as a keepsake. With everyone else so far away, the bits and pieces I'd brought from home were the only things that kept me company: that clown jumper knew what I had been through; it was my friend.

I should have known I was in trouble. Once you start thinking your belongings are companions, there's really no going back. I'd moved to Melbourne but I was living inside my head. Goodness knows what would have become of me if I had not met Adam. Without him, I may well have ended up living in a house full of tin foil and cats, wandering through its rooms, forever murmuring softly to the pictures on my clothes.

Chapter Four

Adam became a solid part of my life towards the end of my first full year of living in Melbourne. We'd met on the set of a student production of *Romeo and Juliet*. I was helping out on the administrative side of things (I was too shy to tell anyone I wanted to be a performer) and Adam was playing the Friar. How anyone could manage to turn a character as pious and earnest as that into a cross between Mr Humphries from *Are You Being Served?* and Riff Raff from *The Rocky Horror Picture Show* is anyone's guess, but Adam did it. He was the loudest, brashest, bravest person I had ever met. I never had the courage to actively befriend him, I just hovered around him long enough that, by the time he noticed me, he simply assumed I was part of his entourage.

From that time on, we wasted enormous chunks of our lives together, watching cable TV, gossiping, window shopping and fighting over the last biscuit in the packet. It was Adam who helped me to acclimatise to life in the big smoke: talking me through the etiquette of nightclubs; teaching me how to ride a tram without falling over; helping me to tell the difference between gay men and straight men. Eventually, I was even confident enough to ride on escalators on my own. With Adam's guiding hand and hilariously acerbic wit, I slowly came out of my shell. I even managed to find myself a boyfriend, much to my own surprise.

His name was Thomas and he was kind, compassionate and funny and he came complete with a broken-down old car he called Gertrude and an equally broken-down old cat he called Santa. I was in awe of him right from the start. He was the most competent person I had ever met and nothing ever frightened him. Any problem I had, he knew how to solve it.

And he loved me.

That, above all else, was the most amazing thing in the world. Here was I, this ridiculous little country bumpkin who hung off the coat-tails of her best friend like her life depended on it and this man loved me. With Thomas by my side, I finally felt like I had found a place in the world.

When I broke up with him three years later, I lost that place again. I was stunned. After three years of watching the way Thomas approached life I was sure that it had rubbed off on me. I was wrong; it turned out I was only confident when he was around. It was Adam who held my hand through the most emotional times and when I moved out of the flat Thomas and I had shared, it was Adam who helped me find a new place to live. Or tried to help. Even Adam couldn't help me find a place big enough to store all of my stuff.

When Thomas and I broke up, I'd volunteered to move out. I felt it was the least I could do, considering I was the one who had ended things. I dragged Adam to countless house inspections until I finally found the only thing I could afford: a piece of crap located just the other side of where anyone would visit. A month later, I'd still not unpacked. I couldn't unpack. There was nowhere to put everything.

One day, as we were sitting in our favourite café and I was complaining for the hundredth time about my lack of storage, Adam finally snapped.

'If you didn't have so much shit, we wouldn't be having this conversation. Again.' Adam tapped his coffee spoon on the table impatiently.

'You've got just as much crap as me, probably more,' I countered.

'That's different.'

27

'How?'

'I don't bang on about it constantly!' He pursed his lips, added another sugar and stirred his coffee. 'I quietly live in my filth and keep my mouth shut.'

The idea of Adam ever keeping his mouth shut made me laugh out loud. I had once witnessed him telling a famous Australian soap-star-turned-pop-star that he had her CD—and did she want it back?

'Adam, I swear you couldn't possibly live in my place either. There's only one cupboard. One cupboard! You'd be in just as much trouble as me.'

'There's a wardrobe, there's the drawers and cabinets in the kitchen, there's under your bed.' He put down his coffee spoon and looked at me seriously. 'There's plenty of room, Corinne. Maybe you should think about getting rid of some of your stuff.'

I looked at him like he'd just announced I should find a random puppy and have it put down.

Secretly, I had no idea if Adam had more stuff than me. Until I'd moved, I hadn't realised how much stuff I had myself. It had built up so incrementally, starting way back when I was still at university. The little grains of my childhood had slowly, almost imperceptibly, migrated down to Melbourne like sand shifting from one beach to another. Every time I went home I'd spy knick-knacks, old clothes or mementos I couldn't live without and I'd bring them back with me. More often than not they never left the box in which I'd packed them for the journey. In the beginning there'd been enough room for all of it. Now, there was barely enough room for me.

When I had started looking for a new place, I had known exactly what I wanted: a big apartment so that I could get all of my things out of storage. Cupboards had been my only prerequisite—not dishwashers or courtyards or gas heating—just cupboards. Thomas had never really known how much I owned. The first place we'd shared was tiny, with barely enough room for a bed and even less for the couch. We'd rented a storage cage until we found somewhere bigger and I'd locked away a stack of boxes without telling him what was in them. Better he thought I had a lot of important documents and family heirlooms than ten-year-old newspapers, broken computers and all of my high-school science projects. Likewise, there was no need for him to know that I had kept all of my socks since primary school. When we finally did move somewhere bigger—a large, sunny one-bedroom flat with floor-to-ceiling storage and a massive, tri-door built-in robe—I still didn't pull my things out of storage. I'd got used to hiding them.

Adam and I had looked at flats for weeks, slowly radiating further and further out from the inner suburbs, trying to find a place with enough storage that was within my budget. We found nothing suitable at all. In fact, even taking the cupboards out of the equation, there simply weren't any flats I could afford on my own in the inner suburbs. I was getting desperate. Living with Thomas had become unbearable for both of us. There is nothing more distressing than having to share a bed with the person you have just broken up with, except for a Celine Dion concert. I would go to bed, hearing him breathe beside me, and it was like I had been knocked over the head with a dull object and stunned. I felt like a fish about to be gutted.

On many of those nights I would close my eyes and will myself not to think about anything. I was scared that if I started to think about what it would be like to live on my own for the first time in my life, I might chicken out and decide to stay. I also didn't want to think about how much pain I was causing Thomas. I had been too cowardly to tell him my real reason for leaving, instead giving him some cliché about us being at different stages in our lives. I didn't want to hurt him with the simple, brutal fact that sometimes it feels more lonely in a relationship than on your own. We'd grown apart and I couldn't see a way to fix it.

Still, lying beside him every night, listening to him breathe and wondering if he was really sleeping or just lying there, stunned and aching like
I was, none of it felt right. It felt like I was severing myself from the best
thing in my life. Thanks to Thomas, I was financially stable for the first
time ever. I had order and rhythm and someone who was there at the end
of every day. I had someone who killed spiders for me and held me when
I cried; Thomas had always fixed the things I couldn't. I thought that I
would be able to do those things for myself once I left, but now, whenever
I thought about life on my own, I went numb with panic. So I thought
about the new flat instead.

Thankfully Adam had been doing an excellent job of distracting me
whenever I started to falter, mainly by saying something ridiculous and
making me laugh, or by taking me out and plying me with ice-cream.
However, he was not helping with the house-hunting in the way I had
hoped he would. As it became more and more apparent that what I wanted
and what I could afford did not share the same postcode—or possibly
not even the same city—I had lowered my expectations. Then I lowered
them again. And again. Adam thought I was being ridiculous; I was now
inspecting places where the walls didn't even meet the floors. We would
walk into a place, I'd look hopefully at Adam and he would mutter 'E.A.D.'
then turn around and walk out. The first time he said it, I grabbed him by
the arm just before he reached the front door.

'What's E.A.D.?'

Adam looked at me over his shoulder, one eyebrow cocked.

'It stands for "Eats A Dick". My sister invented it. If you see something that's shit, like, for example, your shoes or this house, then you say
"E.A.D." Got it?'

I got it. Every house I looked at ate a dick. Some of them ate three or
four dicks and looked like they were suffering not only from the threat
of demolition but also dick-based indigestion. I applied for all of them.

I was always surprised and a little insulted when my application was turned down. When a real estate agent decides you're not good enough to rent a slum, it's hard not to take it personally.

Eventually, after four weeks of solid disappointment, rejection and sleeping in the same bed as my heartbreakingly patient ex-boyfriend, I found a real estate agency that was willing to rent me one of their finest hovels. When I had inspected it, it was full of broken furniture, a broken shower screen and a bathroom so mouldy it was like walking into the Little Mermaid's grotto—if the Little Mermaid had been a sloppy old tart with scant regard for legionnaires' disease. The sinking feeling in my chest told me this was going to be my new home even before I handed in the application form.

The landlord apologised profusely and told me that of course it would be cleaned before I took up tenancy. It wasn't. Two days after moving in I discovered it was also infested with fleas and what I had thought was yellow paint on the walls was really white paint stained yellow with nicotine. As exciting as it was to realise I was living in Hell, nothing compared to then discovering that the five men who lived in the one-bedroom flat next door were running what I strongly suspected was a methamphetamine lab. If I hadn't been so depressed, I probably would have rung the landlord and complained. Instead, I lay down on the old futon that was the only useful thing I had found in the storage cage and stayed there for two days.

And worse than all this, worse than not having Thomas and being covered in flea bites and living in what now appeared to be the inspiration for the television show *CSI*, my new flat had only one cupboard. I spent days just staring at all of the boxes. It never occurred to me to go through them or to throw anything out, instead I hoped that by staring at them and doing nothing that they would . . . I would . . . that maybe . . . I don't know. I was just hoping the problem would disappear.

On one of those miserable days, in a desperate attempt to distract myself from everything, I decided to invent a sliding scale of hoarding. I was procrastinating, I knew that, but I didn't know what else to do. Maybe if I wrote it all down, I'd be able to see where I fitted in the greater scheme of things. Maybe I'd see that things weren't so bad after all.

This is what I came up with:

LEVEL 1: These people are so neat and tidy, it's terrifying. They are possibly aliens. Not only are they not hoarders themselves, they have probably never even met a hoarder. They live in houses that look like they have come straight from the pages of *Vogue Living*. A quick check of their linen cupboard would reveal that all their towels are the same colour and are all folded exactly the same. There is nothing on the kitchen benches—in fact, there is nothing on any of their surfaces except bowls of fruit or flower arrangements or perhaps some kind of weird African artefact reminiscent of something you'd expect to see being used as a murder weapon in a TV crime show. They have a special cupboard just for their kettle. The coffee table holds nothing but one magazine, probably the latest edition of *Vogue Living*.

LEVEL 2: As above but they have bookshelves. It is just possible to discern that the people living here have personalities.

LEVEL 3: Everything is still neat and tidy but a bit more quirky. There is a collection of something—perhaps antique toy cars—displayed in a wooden box with little compartments for each car. There are mixed cushions and throws and framed prints, each accompanied by an anecdote about where it was found or who gifted it. There might be an artfully arranged collection of hardcover books, stacked one on top of the other with a lamp resting on top.

LEVEL 4: Some of the more quirky pieces are starting to look a lot less like artistic statements and more like twenty-first birthday presents the owners do not have the heart to throw out. There is just a little too much furniture in each room and there is stuff hidden under the bed. If there is a copy of *Vogue Living* on the coffee table, it's been there for six months.

LEVEL 5: The pile of books with the lamp on top looks unstable and is in addition to a real lampstand. There are cushions that match nothing and some of them are hideous. One has a picture of cats on it. There is a pile of magazines, various bits of mail and unpaid bills on the coffee table. There is a bowl of random 'things to be fixed' on the kitchen bench. There are magnets smothering the door of the refrigerator holding letters, old cartoons from the back page of the newspaper and out-of-date council notices about hard rubbish collection. There is another refrigerator in the shed. The only note stuck to it reads: 'To be fixed.'

LEVEL 6: To the untrained eye, these houses may not look much worse than the average, slightly untidy suburban home. Just don't open the cupboards or try to put something in the boot of their car. These people have been known to fill their saucepans and casserole dishes with old letters and postcards, pop the lids back on and shove them in a cupboard. The bookshelves contain not only books but paperwork, folders, boxes, ornaments and novelty coffee mugs. There are throws placed over desks and occasional tables to camouflage the piles of paperwork hidden underneath. Opening a cupboard normally involves using a free hand to stop everything falling out. There is a room that no one goes into and no one talks about.

LEVEL 7: One or more family members have had to move out or die to make room for the stuff. Most rooms in the house are unusable and moving around or sitting down involves shifting things. Even the dining chairs are piled with an assortment of crap and the tablecloth is spread in such a fashion as to hide it. There are rusting and broken bits of things in the yard. There is no hiding this amount of stuff and even the neighbours can tell that a hoarder lives next door.

LEVEL 8: As above but add cats.

LEVEL 9: These people have never thrown out anything that might be used again. There is used tin foil, egg cartons, old tins, broken televisions and drawers full of string. Every surface is covered. Often these people have lived through the Depression or were incredibly poor at some point in their lives.

LEVEL 10: These are the people you see on TV. These are the people that either make you feel better about yourself because you are not them, or they petrify you because you are scared you are going to become them.

I carefully reread my scale and looked around my flat. When I had been living with Thomas I was hovering around the lower reaches of Level Five. Now, with everything out in the open, I realised I was scarily close to leaping straight up to a fully fledged Level Seven. I rubbed the back of my neck. I had thought the list would comfort me. Instead, it was giving me heart palpitations.

This spurred me into a kind of panicky action. I made a wall out of the boxes to separate the open-plan lounge and kitchen, threw a rug over the top and convinced myself I was interior decorating. I promised myself that one day I would go through all my photographs and put them in albums, that I would go through the garbage bag of stamps, soak the paper off them and put them in order and that I would go through the little suitcase of moth-eaten doll's clothes, wash and mend them and give them to charity. Then I sat down on the insect-riddled carpet and cried. I avoided the grief of ending a long-term relationship and instead sobbed over a box of unlabelled video tapes.

As time went on, things got slightly better. Adam would visit and fuelled by champagne, we would hammer together bookshelves and a weird little bathroom cabinet that was missing one side. We bought side tables and chests and baskets and eventually we found enough room on the floor to carve a path from the bedroom through the lounge and into the kitchen. Adam thought we'd made a good start. I didn't dare tell him this was as good as it was going to get.

At night I would go to bed and listen to the drug lords either partying or fighting. Sometimes the security door would buzz in the early hours of the morning and after ten minutes of no one answering, I would fly out of bed and let in some obviously high kid and yell at him all the way to his door. They probably thought they lived next door to a dragon who wore Winnie-the-Pooh pyjamas.

In the evenings I would waste my time rearranging and re-stacking piles of god-knows-what, trying to find the magical configuration that would enable me to feel like I was in control. The fear of doing something I might later regret overruled any desire to throw something out. If I threw out an old placemat, I might all of a sudden find myself completely unmoored from my past. If I threw out a cardigan my mother had given to me for my twenty-third birthday, I might destroy the family bond that held us to each other. We don't call our possessions 'belongings' for nothing and without Thomas beside me it felt like my belongings were the only things holding me together.

I tried very hard not to reminisce about how different the place I had lived in with him had been. Our flat had been almost new, with an air conditioner and enormous balcony. It had wooden venetian blinds and polished floorboards. It even had its own entrance, separate to the rest of the apartments, and I never tired of climbing up our little terracotta-tiled staircase, opening the big front gate and stepping onto our decking. We had everything we needed in our little flat: we had new crockery and stainless-steel saucepans, we had a new quilt and fresh linen, we had just the right amount of towels and all of our clothes fitted into the enormous wardrobe with ease. In the house of horrors I now called home, even the blinds were so old they were filled with holes. The blue evening light would shine through them, leaving spooky spots on the walls. It was like living in an eighties music clip.

When I left, Thomas had given me his sofa, his coffee table, a load of kitchen stuff and our doona. Everywhere I looked, there he was. And where he wasn't, there was some other reminder of a life lived years ago. Nothing looked like a life lived now. This wasn't how I had expected it to be. Whenever I couldn't stop myself thinking about it, my mind drifted to imagining Thomas on his own in our old flat and I wondered what it looked like now. Probably clean. And uncluttered. He had always liked new stuff. In a world without me, he would have sat at Level Three. Still, I wondered if he was now doing the same thing I was, wandering aimlessly around our old apartment, rearranging things and trying to pretend there was nothing missing.

I stared at the blue spots of light streaking through the blinds and onto the walls and imagined I really was living in a music clip after all:

Here is Corinne fondling an old pair of pants. Here is Thomas polishing his new car. Here is Corinne hiding seven years' worth of junk under a rug she was given for her twenty-first birthday. Here is Thomas buying a new couch. Here is Corinne listening to her cassette tapes from high school. Here is Thomas buying a stainless-steel coffee maker and a copy of *Vogue Living*. Here are two people on their own, lying in different beds and dreaming of different stuff.

Chapter Five

Months after I had moved out, Thomas and I were still speaking every day, often leaving an awkward pause at the end of the conversation where we used to say 'I love you'. Neither of us wanted to end the friendship and deep down, I was relieved. I couldn't cope on my own just yet, I needed Thomas' good sense and confidence to buoy me up. I didn't feel guilty about it; he still needed me as well and it would have been cruel of me to cut him out of my life completely. Still, there were things I wasn't telling him—like how truly hideous my new flat was. I knew it would only upset him. And besides, I had Adam to complain to about that.

'Oh my god, Adam, if those junkies next door don't shut the hell up, I am going to belt them to death with my rollerskates.'

I was huffing around the house after yet another sleepless night.

'You still have rollerskates?'

Damn, now I'd put myself in it.

'I found them last time I was home. I thought they might come in handy.'

'For what?' Adam sounded incredulous. 'Are you going to re-create a Cliff Richard video clip? Can you even rollerskate?'

I wasn't about to tell him that the skates were actually a child's size seven and I couldn't have fitted into them even if I'd chopped off my toes.

They were sitting next to the couch, all red and white with teeny little wheels. They were too adorable to throw out.

'That's not the point, Adam.'

'Then what is? No. Stop. Forget that. What are you doing this weekend? Do you want to go out somewhere?'

'I can't, I'm going to a birthday party with Thomas. It's for his great-aunt.' I fiddled with the telephone cord. 'She doesn't know we've broken up and it's easier for Tom if she thinks we're still together.'

There was a long pause on the other end of the line.

'You do realise he's your *ex*-boyfriend, don't you?'

'Adam, it's not that simple.'

'Yes it is! Let him go before he thinks you're getting back together.'

'He knows we're not getting back together, he knows that, Adam.'

'Really? Are you sure?'

Bloody hell. I toed the rollerskates. Thomas knew we weren't getting back together; I'd made that clear. We were still friends because we needed each other. Or because I felt guilty for leaving him. Or because he felt bad for becoming distant in our relationship. Or because—oh god. I didn't know. The truth was, I'd never been very good at understanding boys. I'd always missed the signs. Craig in the caravan and Thomas were just two of my disasters.

I looked down at the rollerskates again. When I really thought about it, they didn't make me feel good, they made me feel a little bit guilty. The last time I'd worn them, Shane Doltrey had wound up in hospital.

I was eleven years old and in grade five in Corryong. The whole class was going to the skating rink in Albury–Wodonga and I had been beside myself. *Xanadu* was my favourite movie in the whole wide world and I had watched the closing skating spectacular so many times that the video tape was starting to stretch. I wanted to be Olivia Newton-John in her long flowing seventies frocks and off-the-shoulder shirts. I wanted Zeus as my father and I wanted—oh, how I wanted—to live in a rollerskating rink.

I had been given a pair of white lace-up boot rollerskates with red trim and red wheels for my eleventh birthday and I'd worn them so much that one of my legs had turned out on a weird angle and I couldn't sit cross-legged anymore. I had skated up and down the concrete path to the clothesline for hours every day. I had put my skates on as soon as I got home from school and only took them off again when it was too dark to see where I was going. And yet I never got the hang of it. I couldn't go backwards and I couldn't stop unaided. I had to grab the Hills hoist on my way past, just before I ran out of concrete and hit the grass. I had no talent whatsoever. But I had enthusiasm: blind, avid, weirdly obsessive enthusiasm.

The trip to Albury–Wodonga was going to be brilliant. I had decided on my outfit a week in advance: my best pair of bubble-gum jeans and a lolly-pink cable-knit jumper. The most exciting part about it, however, was not the rollerskating at all, but the opportunity to spend the day trying to get the attention of Shane Doltrey. I loved Shane Doltrey. Everything I did, I did for Shane Doltrey. Does Shane like pink? Of course he does, I should wear the pink jumper. Does Shane like Billy Idol? Yes he does, and he hates the Village People. Best that I memorise all the words to 'Mony Mony' and make sure I don't join in the actions to 'YMCA'. Does Shane like rollerskating? Hard to tell. Perhaps I can teach him and he'll be so impressed, he'll fall in love with me in return. I stayed awake the whole night before we made the trip, wriggling with excitement and inventing all sorts of scenarios that would involve Shane asking me to marry him.

There were some difficulties to overcome in the planning for the big day. For a start, my last romantic encounter with him had not worked out well. I was still too forceful, I didn't understand that romance requires a light touch. I thought if you loved a boy with force, you approached him with force. At that age, the standard way to convey affection was to pull the hair of the object you desired, or give them a punch in the arm or perhaps a kick under the table. Face-pulling and obscene gestures also worked well. I didn't feel that any of those techniques would fully convey the depth of emotion I felt for Shane Doltrey. So instead of relying on something subtle, I borrowed a copy of a hardcover illustrated dictionary from the library and put it in my library bag. Then I waited for Shane Doltrey. When I saw him coming around the corner, I took my library bag and swung it like I was doing the hammer throw. I got him right in the side of his head. I was sure this would express how much I cared about him; I had gone to far more effort than the standard arm pinch or dead leg. Surprisingly, it didn't provoke a marriage proposal, it provoked tears. I was confused, but not disheartened. This was merely the beginning of our little love game. I was laying foundations, and at least now I knew I had his attention. A day of rollerskating was going to clinch the deal.

The morning of the trip we all piled onto the school bus to drive the hour and a half to the city. I didn't get to sit anywhere near Shane Doltrey. He was a back-of-the-bus kind of guy and I was strictly up the front near the teachers, mainly because I had a weird bladder infection that meant I needed to urinate frequently and we had to stop the bus so I could trot off to a public loo every once in a while. I'd made it as far as the middle of the bus on the last trip, but even that was pushing it. There was a hierarchy and there was no point trying to get around it. Of course, if Shane Doltrey and I got married, everything would change, I'd be able to sit where I liked. It would be exactly the same as when Diana married Prince Charles and went from being a child-care worker to rollerskating through Buckingham Palace. See? Even princesses rollerskated!

The first hour on the rink passed without incident. I skated around and I didn't fall over. I even managed a passing resemblance to some backwards skating when I surreptitiously pushed myself off a wall and looked over my shoulder in the professional way I'd seen Gene Pitney do in *Xanadu*. But still, I couldn't catch Shane's attention. In fact, I hadn't seen him on the rink at all. Perhaps he was sitting on the sidelines admiring me from afar. Obviously this wouldn't do, so I got my best friend Leanne to convince Shane's best friend Ben to tell Shane he should put on some skates and go out on the rink. When that didn't work, I dobbed him in to Mrs Allan for not being a joiner and he was forced into it.

And then it happened. I could not have planned anything more perfect. Shane couldn't skate! He was floundering around the edges, trying desperately to stay on his feet and flapping his hands, trying to find something on the wall to hold onto. I could teach him! I could teach him to skate and he would be so impressed he'd forget all about the illustrated dictionary head injury and he'd fall in love with me. But as I skated towards him, something must have frightened him, as he started moving quickly in the other direction. He moved in a way that sort of looked like dog-paddling on land, which wasn't very effective but did mean I could make ground on him fast. Just as I got close enough to call out, he pushed out from the wall and careened into the centre of the rink, grabbing hold of a pylon covered in flashing lights. The pylon was very wide and he couldn't get a very good grip on it and to his horror and my joy, his legs started slowly sliding in opposite directions, creating a sort of splits scenario which even a child as anatomically naïve as I was realised couldn't be the most comfortable position for a boy to find himself in.

Now I had my opportunity. I could rush to Shane's aid and save him from certain pain and humiliation by offering him a steady and skilled hand. But in my haste, I came at him too quickly and for some reason, as he saw me coming, he started trying to slide himself around to the opposite side of the pylon. I changed direction to get at him, he changed direction to get away from me, and we crashed into each other. As he went down, I grabbed one of his arms to pull him up, but to no avail. He crashed heavily on his free arm. He looked bewildered, sort of stunned. He seemed not to notice that I was there at all. His mouth kept opening and closing but no sound came out. And then teachers started running onto the rink. The arm I was holding was fine. But the one on the ground was bent in a decidedly un-arm-like fashion. As Shane didn't seem to notice my presence any longer—no doubt retreating into a world of severe pain—I skated away and left it to the professionals.

In the ensuing mayhem of teachers yelling and ambulances being called, everyone forgot about the part I had played. And later, when the excitement died down and we all got on the bus to go home (leaving Shane at the local hospital), everyone assured me that it wasn't my fault and that I was only trying to help and honestly, if he couldn't skate, why did he go out there in the first place? It was a good point.

I didn't feel much in love with Shane Doltrey after that. A boy who couldn't rollerskate and didn't like the Village People just didn't seem masculine enough.

'Hello? *Hello?* Corinne, are you there? So, what are you going to do? Are you coming out with me on the weekend, or are you going to a party with your ex-boyfriend's family?'

I snapped back to the present. Adam wasn't going to let up. I kicked the skates under the coffee table.

'I'm going to the birthday party.'

Now was not the time to be making rash determinations about the state of my relationship with Thomas. The skates were there to remind me that I was not qualified to make such a decision.

I ended the phone call with Adam, chewed at a fingernail and forced the Thomas problem to the back of my brain. I reasoned that I didn't have time to confront that right now, there was work to be done in the flat, pressing work. My parents had decided to sell the family home (news

I had greeted with all the enthusiasm of someone who had just been told they'd contracted plague) and I would have to go home and clear out my childhood bedroom.

It was obvious that I would have to find room in my flat for all the stuff from home, but so far, I hadn't been able to find anything that I wanted to part with. Today would be a perfect time to start looking again. I got up from the couch and wandered around, fingering things and finding reasons to keep them all. The broken cassette holder I made in year nine? Obviously that couldn't go. You can't throw out something you made yourself, everyone knows that. The collection of half-burnt candles given to me as Christmas gifts by friends I no longer saw? Of course not, they were a testament to the love they had once felt for me; I couldn't heartlessly dump them in a bin. The bubble-gum jeans and lolly-pink cable-knit jumper I wore on the day I went rollerskating with Shane Doltrey? Why was I even asking myself that question? I couldn't even bring myself to throw out the old kitchen curtains from the family home in Corryong. I didn't even realise I had them until I opened a musty box in the back of the wardrobe and there they were, resting on top of a stack of *Smash Hits* magazines. All my childhood memories of that kitchen came slithering out of their bright orange floral print and brought tears to my eyes.

Forgetting that I was supposed to be clearing out, I pulled the curtains from the box, smoothed them out and carried them into the kitchen. I was going to give them a new life. I didn't have curtain rods, so I taped them to the windows. They were full of holes, and because they were taped up instead of hung, they made the kitchen look a little like a shanty town. However, I had made a bit of room in the box. I had somewhere to put the rollerskates now. I smiled. See? I was making progress.

Something vaguely akin to house-pride flared up for the first time since I had moved in. I looked around the lounge room. I owned a cheap second-hand computer desk. It was ugly and I had only bought it as a temporary measure anyway. It held no specific memories. This was something I could easily relinquish and besides, I had another desk on the way. I did not need two desks. It felt very mature coming to that realisation.

The new desk was not really new at all, it belonged to my father, but since he and my mother were moving into a two-bedroom flat, they would not have room for it anymore. I had always coveted it. It was a beautiful roll-top with a wood veneer finish and it came with lockable drawers, an inlaid green leather work surface and a desk calendar from 1977. My crappy grey one paled in comparison. I put up a notice in the landing area of our block of flats advertising my wares. I was so proud of myself, I thought that this must be what it felt like to be a normal person, whatever normal was.

It was weird when I thought about it; I couldn't figure out how other people did it. How did everyone else survive without all of their stuff? I walked back from the landing into my apartment and looked around. Here was Thomas' sofa, here were my grandmother's sauccpans, here were all my cassette tapes from when I was a teenager. Maybe it was because of all of this stuff that I was able to keep going forward. As much as my things annoyed me and took up room and left me with nowhere to sit, I doubted that I could have got by without them. Whenever I felt scared or lonely or unable to cope, there was a book from my childhood or a vase from my mother or an oil burner from an aunt to keep me company. And when even that didn't work, I could distract myself from whatever painful situation I was in by rearranging things and pretending I was tidying up. When other people moved house, they threw things out, gave things away, left things behind. I didn't. I couldn't. When I moved house, I dragged everything along behind me like a snake that should have shed its skin but instead kept it hanging off the end of its tail. And without Thomas by my side, I wasn't about to let go of it all now.

It was the stuff that had got me through the emotional turmoil of the first few months in the new flat. There were so many things about this place that freaked me out. Every morning since moving in I'd been woken by an old man walking past my bedroom window muttering, 'The bastards! The bloody bastards!' He was also short of breath and it would take him upwards of ten minutes to wheeze his way up the two flights of stairs to his apartment every evening. I could hear him over the sound of my stereo, panting and puffing and stopping every now and then to grumble under his breath. His car was parked just near mine and it was impossible not to notice that the rear seats were hidden under a pile of beer cartons and empty wine bottles. I always wondered whether he drank in his car, or if he was just hopeless at getting rid of his recycling.

At first the Bastard Man frightened me. What if he went crazy and started taking his aggression out on the other tenants, namely me? I didn't want to be yelled at or run over by an angry, drunk old man, especially as I didn't have Thomas to protect me. But then—like with the mouldy bathroom, the nicotine-stained walls, the fleas in the carpet and the drug lords next door—because I had my stuff to keep me company, I acclimatised. After coming home to find a police officer out the front of the apartment block yelling, 'Nothing to see here, please move inside quickly' on three separate occasions, an old man's fruity language at 7.30 every morning stopped registering as anything more than a convenient alarm clock.

Just as well.

It was the Bastard Man who answered the advertisement for my desk.

I didn't know whether to celebrate or hide the breakables. I sat waiting for him in my lounge room nervously clenching and unclenching my fists and wondering if he would stomp in and start calling me a bastard as well.

When I opened the door to his knock I saw an old man, tall, stooped, wearing a narrow-brimmed felt hat similar to the ones my uncles wore and exactly the same as the ones that old blokes have been wearing since the fifties. He had on a tweed jacket and grey pants and if I hadn't known about his colourful language and boozy car, I would have said that he was a churchgoer. As it stood, I assumed he probably went to the races a lot.

Thankfully, he turned out to be lovely, in a short-tempered, brusque, slightly addled kind of way, and the first thing he mentioned when he walked into my flat was that his wheezing was caused by emphysema. I hadn't asked about it, I guess he just wanted to tell me so that I wouldn't ask him to carry the desk up the stairs himself. We agreed on a price and he signed a cheque for me in his laborious old man's handwriting, taking care to form each letter as clearly and accurately as he could. Without knowing how I would do it, I promised him that I would have his new purchase delivered.

After two days of staring at the desk and still not figuring out how to get it up the stairs on my own, I hit upon the idea of getting one of the guys from the methamphetamine lab to help. Obviously they didn't volunteer—they didn't even answer the door when I knocked. Instead, I forced them into philanthropy via entrapment.

It was a weekend and I didn't have much on. Knowing I had hours to spare, I grabbed a magazine and dragged the desk out in front of their flat, blocking their doorway. I sat on it, flicking through pictures of celebrities without make-up, until one of them came out and discovered me, smiling politely and jamming their exit. Thankfully, the dopey-looking kid standing in front of me looked too wobbly on his feet to attempt an argument and so, his bloodshot eyes filled with resentment, he helped me carry the desk up the stairs. He disappeared wordlessly as I knocked on the Bastard Man's door.

Without my little meth friend to help me, I had to drag the desk into the flat on my own, backwards. When I had finished and turned around to face the interior of his apartment, it took me a moment to comprehend what I was looking at. I was in one of those places you only ever see on current affairs shows, the kind of story where the camera pans over a vast wasteland of junk and the voiceover says, *sotto voce*, 'Somebody actually lives here.' I had met my first Level Ten.

There was not a spare surface in the flat. The kitchen tables were piled high with yellowing newspapers. The floors were covered in books and boxes and pots and pans and everything imaginable. Everywhere. There was stuff everywhere. The walls were mildewed and there were little insects circling above my head. We put the desk in the kitchen because it was the only place it would fit. He asked me to stay for a drink and I didn't feel that I could say no. So we sat and drank some beers and watched a lifestyle programme that was not to his liking because, as he put it, all the ladies on the show were 'large and horsey, like they should all be spending their time in paddocks rubbing up against tree stumps'. No doubt they were bastards too, he just didn't say it out loud because there was a lady in the room.

We talked about the war, the uselessness of young people, how the new skate park up the road was encouraging hooliganism and about his family. His grandfather had been the person responsible for introducing cane toads to Australia. Or prickly pear. Or some sort of spider. I was not listening as hard as I should have been as I was too busy concentrating on shallow breathing so that the mildew in the flat would not penetrate too deeply into my lungs.

We sat and watched the TV in silence for a while. Some blond guy with big muscles was hammering together one of those useless things they make on those shows, like a rotating shoe rack or a cat massager. Then out of nowhere the Bastard Man told me that his children didn't talk to him anymore. He hadn't spoken to his son or grandchildren in years. He didn't say why, he just said he wasn't invited for Christmas. I felt awkward. Normally the person blathering on about their private life was me. I didn't quite know what to do when a stranger started doing it, especially an old guy. I didn't know if the rules were different. Should I give him advice?

Or should I just sip my beer and point out that another horsey-looking woman was on the TV? I chose the latter. Poor old bugger, I thought. He'd probably bought the desk as an excuse to meet someone in the apartment block.

I stayed for perhaps an hour. The Bastard Man owned a lot of books and as I went to leave, he lent me one about a woman who married a Tibetan nomad and went to live with his family on the plains of Tibet. I was touched. As someone who likes to hold on to their stuff, I realised what an honour it was to be lent something of his. I guessed it was his way of making sure that I visited again: I would have to return the book when I finished reading it. To my way of thinking, you had to be pretty lonely to risk losing your stuff in return for a little company.

I made my goodbyes, wandered down to my flat again, cleared some space on the coffee table and plonked the book down on top of a pile of local newspapers I had not yet got around to reading. I looked at the space where the desk used to be, imagining it filled with the new one, and thought about all the stuff I would be able to cram into its drawers and under its roll-top. I looked around at the walls I had laboriously scrubbed back to white. The fleas had long gone and the only insects that ever came into my flat now were little summertime flies. 'See?' I thought to myself. 'I am nothing like the Bastard Man.'

The house-pride continued. Fuelled by the Bastard Man's beers, I felt brave enough to open a box labelled 'miscellaneous' and start sifting through it. I found a few blank sheets of paper and some old gift wrapping that, with much effort, I relinquished to the recycling bin. But then a crinkled pattern of little Holly Hobby faces stared mournfully up at me from amongst the newspapers and cardboard boxes and I couldn't bear how lonely they looked. In the end I pulled the wrapping back out again and put it in a bag I labelled 'Spare paper for wrapping presents when you can't find where you've put the good paper'.

The rest of the box mostly contained stuff from the early eighties. I spent the evening poring over my primary school-era handwriting, trying to pick out the words in drafts of letters to relatives that I must have written when I was eight years old. The handwriting was almost illegible and disturbingly identical to my handwriting now.

I deciphered each note as best I could, then smoothed it out and put it in the 'keeping' pile. The pile for throwing out contained some rusty bobby pins. When I was done, I repacked the box. I guess it was at that point that I accidentally dropped the Bastard Man's book in there as well. I taped the carton shut without realising and put it back in the wardrobe.

Looking back, I can't believe I didn't miss that book. I didn't miss it then and I didn't miss it when I moved out. It just disappeared and never crossed my mind again.

Until it was too late.

Part 2
Where It Became Unsteady

Chapter Six

Two days later I was back in Corryong sifting through my childhood. I'd left Melbourne that morning after an early breakfast with Adam and a warning from him not to bring too much back with me.

'Here. This is to stop you from acting like an idiot.'

He dropped a Saint Christopher's medallion onto my plate of eggs and bacon. I picked it out and squinted at him suspiciously.

'Adam, what's this got to do with anything? For a start, you're not Catholic, and for another thing, Saint Christopher is the patron saint of travellers. Besides, I'm pretty sure he was de-sainted, or whatever you call it, quite a while ago.'

Adam rolled his eyes.

'Jesus, all right Perry Mason, calm down. I was trying to find you a patron saint for possessions but there isn't one. So then I thought I'd get you one of the Archangel Michael, but I couldn't find one of those either, so—'

'What's he got to do with anything?'

'He's the patron saint of the possessed.'

'Oh, you're hilarious. You're truly, truly hilarious.'

Adam flicked his wrist.

'I know. So in the end I got you a Saint Christopher. He can look after your car and stop you filling it with crap.'

'Except that he doesn't exist.'

'Well they shouldn't keep selling his medallion then, should they? Stupid Catholic church. Well, actually, I got it in one of those two-dollar shops.'

I slipped the little medallion into my purse.

'You do realise you've completely blown your argument by *giving* me crap instead of telling me to get rid of what I've already got, don't you?'

'Haven't you left yet?'

I hugged him goodbye, left him to pay the bill as punishment for being a smartarse, and started the journey back home.

Six hours later I was on my hands and knees on my bedroom floor in Corryong, contemplating a little ball of crumpled paper that, when unfolded, seemed to be a two-page essay titled 'The first thing I am going to talk about is little sisters. Bad points and good'. It was dated to when I was ten years old.

My sister Wendy is two years younger than me and whenever anyone asks (which isn't all that often), I've always likened our childhood to that of Laura and Mary Ingalls in *Little House on the Prairie*. They lived in the country, so did we. They were sisters, so were we. They were partial to pinafores, so were we. We were exactly like them except for the fact that we had running water and an indoor toilet and virtually no trouble from wolves. And neither of us was blind. Like all siblings, we had our disagreements and there was one particularly heated exchange where I lost a chunk of hair, leaving a bald spot on my head about the size of a twenty-cent piece, but on the whole, we were very close. Or so I'd thought.

The weird syntax of the essay—of putting 'bad' before 'good'—gave me an indication that the list was going to be perhaps less than flattering to my sister. Another indication was that the 'bad points' list filled an entire page and the 'good points' list was blank. I started to read it with trepidation.

BAD POINTS

Mess up bedroom

Hang around you

Hang around your friends

Take your things without asking

Then break the things

Say embarrassing things about you

Never get into trouble

Get what they want all the time

Don't feed the cat

Annoy you on purpose

Take all the good posters out of *TV Week*.

In my defence, I hadn't made a single spelling mistake.

Instead of ringing Adam (who no doubt would have told me to throw it out), I rang Thomas. He laughed when I read the list out to him.

'The good posters out of *TV Week*? I've seen your childhood bedroom, remember; neither of you had any good posters.'

'I think she took the one of Bros that I wanted.'

He laughed again. 'Where'd you find it?'

'The list? In a drawer. It just fell out of an old diary.'

I was lying. I had found it beneath a pile of training bras, old copies of *Dolly* and what appeared to be disintegrating hair bobbles, all of which I had carefully put in my 'keeping' pile.

'Hey, guess what? I forgot to tell you, Mum and Dad are selling the house. I'm up in Corryong right now.'

'Really? Wow. Cleaning out that bedroom is going to be a nightmare.'

The first time I had taken Thomas home to meet my family had not gone well. I was nervous about taking him to the country, I was nervous about him meeting my parents for the first time and I was nervous about him seeing my childhood bedroom. To mitigate things I had taken Adam along too, as well as another friend named Jamie. Jamie and I were doing a show together and I was using the trip as an excuse for us to film some footage to use in a sketch. Jamie was a country boy himself, so I thought he could help smooth the way.

The boys were all staying at the local caravan park, but on our first night in town, my fancy new city boyfriend was coming to meet my family on his own. Mum had whipped up a roast and her famous pavlova. We were even using the dining room, the good cutlery and the good table-cloth, all of which were normally reserved for Christmas Day. At the age of twenty-four, this was the first time I had brought a boy home and no one really knew how to react. I am sure that as we were waiting for him to arrive, a small part of my parents wondered whether he might turn out to be imaginary.

Thomas pulled into our driveway exactly on time and the introduc-tions went well. Then Dad and Thomas went out into the backyard for a chat. My sister, my mother and I set the table, smoothed our skirts and generally tried to ignore the fact that I had grown up and was very clearly having sex with someone.

No matter how nervous Thomas had told me he was feeling before he turned up, I knew I was feeling worse. He would eventually want a tour of our house and my childhood bedroom. It still looked the same as the day I had left, complete with the beds made in case we ever needed them. Even our childhood cot was ready to be slept in, presumably in case either of us shrunk. All our toys were still in the toy box and all the ornaments covering our dressing table sat there gathering dust. Piles of my old schoolwork covered the tops of the drawers, posters spilled out of containers and an Itty Bitty Bin full of erasers sat at the foot of my bed. If Dickens' Miss Havisham had grown up a teenager in the eighties and shared a bedroom with her sister, this is what it would have looked like. When Thomas opened the door, I lied and told him that most of the stuff belonged to Wendy.

We sat down to dinner and Dad carved the roast. My father is a very traditional man with some very strong, albeit unusual, rules: shoes should always be shined, men do not swear in front of women, and under no circumstances should fruit ever be put in a savoury dish. Thomas had good shoes and had never shown a penchant for apricot chicken but he came from the city and had a lot of Scottish friends; swearing was like breathing to him. Sure enough, somewhere between the lamb being served and the gravy being poured, Thomas took a call on his mobile at the dinner table and said 'Fuck.' Loudly. Then he said it again. My sister, my mother and I all stared at our plates, hoping that if we did not look up, then the world would conveniently stand still and my father would somehow suffer a very specific form of amnesia, wiping the last ten seconds from his memory. When I eventually did look at my father it was obvious that was not the case. He was still passing around the gravy but he looked like he was passing a stone. Thomas continued his phone call, oblivious to the silent, slow-motion mayhem unfolding around him. I can only imagine that my father decided not to haul Thomas outside and run him down with the rotary hoe because he didn't want his dinner to go cold.

When I told Thomas later what he had done he went weak and had to sit down. So much for first impressions. It would be another year before Thomas finally felt that he had earned my father's forgiveness and that was only because my father accidentally ran into his car and tore off the back end. It was the first and only time I have ever seen someone relieved to be in a car accident.

The next morning my sister Wendy and I drove out to the caravan park to pick up the others. She was still laughing.

'He said "fuck" at the dinner table, Corinne! Maybe we can get him to say grace tonight. "Hey, God, thanks for the fucking chicken."' More laughter.

Adam came running out of the caravan as we parked. 'Jamie knows the bull spoof guy!'

What a wonderful trip this was turning into.

'The bull spoof guy! J went to school with him!' Adam was waving excitedly as if he had just found out that Jamie was related to Mariah Carey.

'We saw him on the telly! He's selling bull spoof!' Adam was laughing maniacally. I could not figure out if Thomas looked amused or sick.

I shut the car door and kissed my boyfriend hello. 'They sell bull semen to farmers for breeding. It's not some kind of weird sex thing. At least not until J and Adam found out about it.'

Jamie grinned. The part of a country kid that delights in grossing out city people never disappears. When I was in high school I made a video for my city penpal that showed me sticking my arm into a cow's mouth to prove they didn't bite. (The cow did bite—a lot—but we managed to edit that out.) Now Jamie, like a true country kid, was standing in the doorway of the caravan, arms folded and laughing as Adam breathlessly told my unimpressed sister everything he had just discovered about artificial animal insemination.

I watched as Jamie climbed into the back of my sister's car. Although we were both from country Victoria, a childhood desire to disturb city people was where the similarities between us ended. He had done a far better job of assimilating into city life than I had. He was groovy. He had groovy wavy blond hair, long, but not too long, just groovy. He wore T-shirts bearing the names of indie bands. He had an earring. Admittedly, he also drove a Barina with cow-print seat covers, so the transformation wasn't complete, but he was a long way ahead of me. I had turned up that morning in a flannel shirt, track pants and

Blundstones. I looked like I should be heading out to a paddock to col-
lect bull spoof myself.

Jamie was the only one in our party that I was not worried about.
Adam was a constant source of concern for too many reasons to list and
Thomas had already proven himself a disaster. Jamie was supposed to be
the one who was in control. So it took us all by surprise when he proved to
be the most unfit for country living out of all of us.

That morning, we were going to visit the local trout farm. Thomas
had never seen a trout farm before and Adam thought it would be funny.
Wendy and Jamie came along, acting as nonchalant as possible. Trout
were nothing special; only city folk got excited about fish. So we went
and we looked at ponds and we saw some fish flapping about. Adam and
Wendy went off to hire some rods and Thomas took a call and went off
to say 'fuck' a lot in private.

I was quite proud of the trout farm. It was one the town's biggest tourist attractions and it sold a trout pâté to which I am yet to find an equal.
It even had an underwater viewing platform where you could watch the
trout swimming about undisturbed. Jamie and I went down for a look.
The viewing area was not perhaps as spectacular as I had remembered it.
It was smaller and murkier. It was pretty much a thirty-centimetre-square
piece of thick glass looking into some cloudy water. Jamie complained
that he couldn't see anything and pressed his face right up to it to get a
better look.

Essentially, a fish is nothing more than a shiny, smelly muscle with a
flipper on each side. Muscles move quickly. Jamie should not have been
at all surprised when one of them shot into view right in front of his
face. Even so, he screamed so loudly that the fish, stunned into uncon-
sciousness, instantly turned upside down and floated to the surface. After
a moment of standing completely still and open-mouthed, we both ran up
the stairs to see if we could find it. Adam came running towards us.

'What happened? Corinne, are you all right? Why were you screaming?'

'It wasn't me, it was Jamie. He screamed at a trout and we think he killed it.'

'What do you mean, "Jamie screamed at a trout"? Who's scared of trout? Jamie? Did you scream at a trout?'

'It came out of nowhere!'

'You're at a trout farm, it didn't come out of nowhere, it came out of a trout pond. Why did you scream at a trout?'

And then we saw it floating on the surface. Jamie put his head in his hands. Then, just as quickly as it had stopped moving, it started again. It was like someone had pushed a reset button and it swam away as if nothing had happened.

Everyone was quiet. Then my sister, standing behind us and holding all the fishing gear, called out, 'Hey, J, how about we forget about these rods and bait and we just let you wade out into the middle of the pond to scream until all the trout float to the surface? You'll be like an aquatic version of Shelley Duvall in *The Shining*.' Adam clapped his hands in delight.

Later that day I took us for a drive somewhere dry, where the fish couldn't hurt us. We drove out the other side of town, my sister and I pointing out the sights along the way. Here's the cemetery that everyone's forgotten about, here's the place that was nearly the capital of Australia, here's the place that was used in a movie once. As we were driving, I saw something in the middle of the road, and as we got closer, I realised it was a turtle. The middle of the road is not a good place for a turtle to be hanging out. Cars are fast, turtles are slow. I pulled over to the side of the road with the plan of picking it up and putting it back onto the grass, safe from oncoming traffic. I will also admit, I had never touched a turtle and I could not envisage a time in the near future when I might get to touch one again. It was an opportunity too good to pass up.

Everyone got out of the car to watch and stretch their legs, which unfortunately made them witnesses to what happened next. I had parked right beside the turtle, so any cars coming along the same side of the road would have to swerve into the centre to get around me. And in the centre of the road was my new little reptilian friend. Where car tyres were once safely passing either side of it, they were now going to go straight over the top. I realised this about a second before a car did exactly that. The turtle took a direct hit and skittered across the road like a gruesome tiddlywink. Now it was my turn to scream. And then I cried. I'd never killed anything before and now, in what was supposed to be my shining Harry Butler moment, I had murdered a turtle.

Perhaps I overreacted. I think I mentioned that I should go to the police station and confess. We all got in the car and drove back to my parents' house. Everyone was stone quiet until Wendy started chanting, 'Corinne killed a turtle, Corinne killed a turtle . . .' Thomas laughed louder than anyone else. I lost my mind and yelled at him, 'Shove it up your arse, fuck boy!' Everyone laughed even harder.

Now, back in Corryong again and talking to him on the phone, I was missing Thomas terribly. I was missing everything terribly. Thomas, Jamie, Adam, my childhood, everything. I was spiralling down into a vortex of sentimentality and I had to end the phone call quickly before I told him that I wished he was with me.

This was all just to do with packing, I told myself. Along with all the dust, I was stirring up a whole lot of emotions. I just needed to calm down and focus on what I was doing. The problem was, what I was doing was making things worse. Moments of extreme emotion were coming thick and fast. How was I going to throw any of this out? I was sifting through it, cherishing it, fondling it and reminiscing about it. Everything, down to the woollen beanie with the pompom ties that my sister wore when she was three, was bringing tears to my eyes. Wendy was picking stuff up, shoving it in bags and throwing it out. She was making huffing sounds every time she looked in my dewy-eyed direction. No wonder. I was sitting in a pile of Fido Dido T-shirts and Cherry Lane singlets remembering my first ever Blue Light Disco and softly singing the lyrics to 'Maniac'.

The only things I had managed to turf were two skivvies, one maroon and the other bottle-green, and even those I photographed before discarding. And when Wendy wasn't looking, I carefully rolled up her Bros poster, stuck it in a cylinder and secreted it away in the boot of my car.

When we were kids, Wendy's and my tastes were worlds apart and neither of us approved of the other. Wendy preferred the crass commerciality of a Mickey Mouse T-shirt or a pair of Garfield shorts. I, being older and wiser, shunned her fashion-enslaved sensibilities and instead preferred to wear whatever took my fancy. Consequently, I often wanted to wear pink trousers and team them with things with pictures of spaceships on them. Sure, Wendy may have looked stylish and hip and up to the minute, but I was comfortable and that was what mattered.

I did once accidentally buy something fashionable, a 'Choose Life' T-shirt. Of course I was completely unaware that it had anything to do with Wham!, I just liked the pink writing on the front. (I was holding it again now, smoothing out the wrinkles and remembering the denim pedal pushers that had completed the ensemble.) But even when I was wearing that T-shirt Wendy was still far ahead of me, with a red crop-top and white plastic hoop-earrings that looked like the whites of a sliced boiled egg with the yolk popped out. She was a little Anglo-Saxon, pre-adolescent version of Grace Jones. She was the Skipper to my Barbie. She was the one who looked like fun.

I snuck out to the shed where Wendy had made her pile to go to charity and reclaimed the red crop-top. Perhaps she was able to let it go, but I couldn't. It was etched into my memory and summed up the essence of my little sister.

I wish I could say that sentimentality was my only reason for taking that top. I know I believed that at the time; I even chastised myself for being silly and I knew that Wendy would roll her eyes if she saw what I was doing. But when I was out in the shed, before I stashed it away in my car, I'm ashamed to say that I tried it on. The only thing sadder than a twelve-year-old trying to look cool is a thirty-year-old woman trying to look like a twelve-year-old trying to look cool. When I came back into the bedroom, I tried to act as nonchalant as possible, but I'm sure there was a glittery lunacy to my expression that was betraying me.

The day was not going well. I'd been trying to ignore it, but everything felt wrong. There was a pounded-down grief in the room that was almost suffocating me and I couldn't find where it was coming from. I kept carting things out to my car and taking deep breaths of hot summer air but nothing helped. It felt like there was something in the room that was unspeakably sad and while I was scared to find it, I was equally scared that I wouldn't.

When the packing ended, my sister and I parted on gruff terms. She was pissed off with my sentimentality and I was pissed off with myself as well. I didn't tell her that though; she was my sister. I blamed her instead. We wound up having a terrible fight and I left, each of us vowing never to speak to the other again. At that stage neither of us knew that promise would only last a week.

Driving back to Melbourne I could feel my hands shaking on the steering wheel. There was something terribly wrong. I didn't seem to be able to breathe. I counted down the kilometres until I passed the old pine forest that marked the edge of the boundary of my childhood world. I pulled over to the side, staggered from my car and collapsed in the grass with snot pouring down my face. I had never felt so physically torn apart by grief. I couldn't move. I just lay in the long grass, face down, hidden from the road by my car, and screamed into the dirt. It was like my bones had gone. I had lost my family home, I had lost my sister, I had lost my boyfriend.

When I was able, I got back in the car, drove a little further to the edge of the Hume Weir, got out and sat by the shore, my face swollen and red and just a little bit covered in grass. I was looking for another turtle. I wanted to see something special. I wanted to see something self-contained. I wanted to see something I hadn't ruined.

Chapter Seven

I had arrived home late after the trip to Corryong, dragging one box into the house and leaving the rest in the car. I cleared a space on my bed and lay down amongst newspapers, coats and what probably used to be a sandwich. I knew I should finish emptying out the car, I knew I should make some room in the house for the boxes that were about to come in, I knew I should get whatever wet thing I was lying on out from underneath me, and yet I couldn't do any of it. All I could do was lie on my side and stare at the wardrobe door, thinking about the crap lurking on the other side. I was a complete failure.

I thought about ringing Thomas and asking for his help but stopped myself just in time. Maybe Adam was right, maybe I was relying on Tom too much. Then again, every day that I didn't call him, I felt bad for abandoning him. I rubbed my eyes. This was a quandary I was in no fit state to consider. Even on a good day I would have had trouble with it, let alone on a day like today, when I was a floppy mess and I wasn't sure why. I rolled onto my back, stared at the ceiling and took stock of what might be causing me to feel so bad. There was the loss of the family home, there was the stuff in the car, there was the stuff in the flat, there was the fight with my sister, and yet the problem didn't seem to be any of that. It felt like something bigger and scarier. The problem was that I didn't know what the problem was. I rang Adam.

'Hey.'

'Hey, honey. You sound miserable.'

'I am.'

'Do I need to come around with a bottle of wine?'

'No. Just tell me something outrageous and make me laugh.'

We reminisced about Corryong, the fish and the bull spoof guy, and I hinted that the fight with Wendy might have been why I was so upset.

'I don't think that's it at all, Corinne.' Adam was in full psychiatrist mode and I imagined he was pacing his lounge room, gesticulating as he spoke. 'I think you've just spent a weekend dredging up your past and you're feeling vulnerable. The good thing is, it's over now. You'll wake up tomorrow and feel fine.'

He didn't know about all the stuff. He didn't know that I had packed so much into my hatchback that the only space left was around the accelerator and brake pedals. He didn't know that I had filled my car to the brim with guilt and then parked it outside my flat. And he didn't know that one object in particular was haunting me worse than everything else: an oversized piece of exercise equipment my father had given me for Christmas ten years previously.

Like most fathers, Dad left the gift-buying to Mum, so it was always a big deal when he came up with an idea himself. On Christmas morning 1987, after breakfast and the obligatory phone calls to relatives, we sat down to open our gifts. Dad was grinning with anticipation as I ripped off the paper to find a large box emblazoned with the French title *Le Marchepied #1 Step!*, or *The Super Step*, as the helpful translation said beneath.

Le Marchepied #1 Step! was essentially a platform that rested on four separate feet (or *pieds* as those fancy French folk would say) that could be heightened or lowered depending on your fitness level. It also came with an instructional video for step aerobics, presented by Brenda Dykgraaf, a

US aerobics champion who, if the shiny tan stockings and high-cut, hot pink leotard were anything to go by, knew what she was doing. In terms of being up to date, my father had it spot on: it was the eighties and aerobics was all the rage. In terms of impressing his fickle teenage daughter, he'd missed the mark completely.

A good daughter would have been thrilled to receive such a thoughtful gift, and even if it wasn't exactly what she was after, she would have enthusiastically pulled it out of its box, popped on the video and jumped around the living room, whacking her knees to her elbows, and yelling, 'I feel the burn!' Instead, I rolled my eyes. I didn't even inwardly giggle at the name 'Dykgraaf'.

'Put it on and have a try,' my mother encouraged. She knew what was up. She knew nothing would thrill Dad more than to see his daughter bouncing around like a slightly less girly version of Richard Simmons while panting out an earnest, 'Thanks, Dad, this is brilliant! Happy Christmas to you too!' But I was fourteen. I was a turd.

I reluctantly stuck the video in the machine, hit the play button and made a great show of how exhausting it all was. I heaved up and down on the step, wincing and puffing as if I was an arthritic eighty year-old. Brenda Dykgraaf bounced along on screen, shouting out instructions and grinning iridescently. I scowled back at her. How dare she expect normal people to find this kind of torture enjoyable—what did she think I was, an idiot? Who in their right mind would voluntarily endure this kind of pointless up-and-down puffy stuff in their lounge room on a regular basis? The more I did it, the more I started to believe that I was a martyr and I was being asked to do something unreasonable. I think I even faked a cramp to further illustrate my point. Eventually my mother snapped that if I didn't want to do it, then I should stop carrying on and just pack the damn thing away.

I didn't feel vindicated, I felt childish. However, instead of letting that show, I dismantled it, slid it back into its packaging and sulkily kicked it under my bed, knowing it could take the abuse because it said on the box that it was *solide et robuste*. I never used it again.

Back in Corryong cleaning out the house, I had found it under my bed. Although a little dusty, the box was undamaged and Brenda was still there on the cover, still smiling and resting one foot on top of *Le Marchepied* as if it were a mountain peak she had just conquered. But her expression was no longer inviting or encouraging. Now she seemed to be saying, 'I am the ghost of Christmas Past. You don't love your father.' I immediately lugged it out to the car. Guilt is portable.

I vowed to myself that once I had *Le Marchepied* back in Melbourne I would use it every day. Or maybe twice a week. Or at least once a week. Or whenever I had the time. Whatever the case, this coming Christmas I would arrive home, toned and buff and my father would comment on how good I looked and I would hug him and say, 'It's all thanks to you, Dad, all thanks to you.' The End. Credits Roll. However, now, lying on a sandwich on my bed, I knew that wouldn't happen. For a start, there wasn't even enough room on the lounge room floor to use it.

I nearly told Adam all of that. Nearly. But I was scared he'd laugh at me. There was a slim chance he was right and that I'd wake up tomorrow feeling better so there was no point making myself look ludicrous now. I told him I loved him and hung up the phone. Then I stayed where I was on the bed until I fell asleep.

The next morning I wandered around the lounge room and tried to figure out where I could fit the new stuff. There was some room behind the fridge and I hadn't used all the space under the coffee table yet. I remembered how Jamie used to joke that he used his oven as a filing cabinet—maybe I could do that as well. I'd just have to limit myself to stove-top cooking. I carried in everything else from the car and set it down in the part of the lounge room that usually served as the pathway to the kitchen. It was a big pile and I stared at it hopelessly. Now it was inside, I realised there was absolutely no way I had room for any of it. I sighed and rubbed my eyes. I was going to have to clean out the wardrobe.

I dragged myself into the bedroom like I was about to face my own execution. I opened the wardrobe and like the truly gutless person I was, I started with the sock drawer. Perhaps if I could part with some old worn-out socks, I would have room for the new old worn-out socks I had brought back from Corryong. Over the next two hours I managed to ditch two pairs. I didn't even unroll them first and play sock puppets. It was hard and it was miserable and I hated letting them go.

I went back out to the lounge room, sat on the floor and stared at the pile in front of me. Every little skerrick of my childhood was there. I knew that I was the sum of all my experiences but really, did I need to keep everything so that I could relive those experiences whole? It appeared that I did. Why then could other people happily throw their stuff away and not disintegrate? How did they make decisions about what to let go of and what to keep? And why the hell wasn't anyone telling me how they did it?

Something snapped. Now I just wanted to chuck something out, anything. Not the stuff in front of me though—that was my precious childhood—something else would have to go. I grabbed a chair, dragged it back into the bedroom, reached to the top of the wardrobe and dragged down two massive storage bags. They were too heavy to lift out properly so I simply dropped them from full height. One of them glanced off the dressing table and slumped like a body, half sitting against the mirror and half sprawled across the floor. I climbed down from the chair and kicked its carcass to the ground, ripped it open and started pulling out its guts. I made a furious, random decision that neither of those bags was going back up.

Things moved swiftly; I'd started with the right bag. It was full of old T-shirts and stuff that I didn't really care for anymore. It didn't hurt to let go of it, it was more a case of wondering why it was still there. It was unbelievably and deliriously easy: keep, give away, keep, give away, give away, give away, give away. I couldn't believe it: I didn't want most of this stuff. I could live without it. Then it really hit me. Oh my god! I could live without it! What I'd been fearing all this time was completely unsubstantiated, there was nothing in here that I wanted, it all should have gone years ago and hadn't, not for any real reason but simply because I was disorganised and slack. I finished sorting through the bag in less than an hour, keeping only two things. Then I opened the other one. This was exhilarating! I'd discovered the secret! I was succeeding! I was—Uh-oh.

These were all the clothes that I had worn when I first left home. Instantly I was transported back in time and I was eighteen years old again, in a share-house in Albury–Wodonga, the year before I moved to Melbourne. I was standing in the first bedroom I had ever had to myself, wearing these faded purple leggings and this hand-knitted jumper. I kept going through the bag and everything I touched became a time machine; I was getting dressed up, putting on these blue jeans and this black knitted top to go dancing at The Basement, where Waltons department store used to be. I pulled out a little pair of cherry-shaped earrings and now I was with my best-going-out-girlfriend Lara and we were dancing to our self-proclaimed theme song, Mel and Kim's 'Respectable'; she was wearing her tight Lee jeans and bodysuit, I was wearing my trusty leggings and jumper. I delved further into the bag and now I was at my sister's debutante ball—thinking myself a sophisticated city chick—wearing this bottle-green knee-length skirt and matching vest, topped off with a frilly white shirt and golden heart-shaped locket the size of the clock worn by Flavor Flav. I stuck my hand into the bag again and now I was standing in the dark, just off Dean Street, after traipsing from one nightclub to another, hoping against hope that I would meet up with the boy I was madly in love with and now, in an alleyway and wearing this cream pirate shirt with these brown string laces, I was holding his hand and he was just about to kiss me for the first time. How could I let go of all these memories? Of pimple remedies and straightening my hair with a clothes iron (and accidentally burning the tips of my ears), of learning to cook lasagne from the recipe we found on the back of a cheese packet, of living away from home for the first time and the frisson that ran through me for a whole year: 'I've got my own room!' 'I'm in charge of my life!' 'This is the start of what it's like to be an adult!' Nothing would ever beat the excitement of that time, when everything was ahead of me and I didn't care what that everything was. I held those clothes in my hands and I wasn't a miserable, lonely woman living in a flat full of crap anymore, I was someone with hope.

There was no way I was throwing any of this out.

I put the bag I was going to get rid of at the foot of my bed and the other one back where I had found it. There was no sense in rushing these things, I told myself. There was no point in working myself up into a state and doing something I would regret.

I could smell the failure.

I looked in the wardrobe again. I was hoping I would find some big thing I could throw out, something that I had missed every other time I'd opened these doors. I looked properly this time, not half-heartedly—and then I saw it. There was a garbage bag right down the bottom, underneath an old single-bed doona. I had vague recollections of filling that bag years ago—back before I was living with Thomas—and then never giving it away, presumably for the same reasons I wasn't letting go of the newly filled one now. I stared at it and thought hard. Whatever was inside I had already decided to let go of once, and obviously I wasn't missing it. I quickly grabbed it and threw it into the hallway. Once it was out of the closet, there was room for *Le Marchepied* to slot in and because it was such a flat, sturdy box I could pile other things on top of it. By the time I was done rearranging and repacking the wardrobe, almost everything I had brought back with me from Corryong was crammed in. I couldn't believe it. I stared at the bag lying in the hall. Before I could change my mind, I picked it up and headed out to the car. I was going to dump it on the passenger seat, start the ignition and drive straight to a charity shop. I was grinning like an idiot. I was finally letting go of something, not because I had come to terms with saying goodbye to the bag's contents, but because I'd forgotten what was in it. This had to be the secret to letting go that everybody else already knew about.

I rang Adam before I drove off. My call went through to voicemail, so I left a message telling him that he was right, I had woken up feeling better today and in fact, I felt so much better that I was starting a project to clear out my life. I went on and on about how amazing I felt, how exhilarating it was to be taking control of my life, how great it felt to unburden myself. I was burbling—I knew that—but without him on the other end of the line to pull me back from the edge, I was off on a flight of fancy.

I was sitting in my hatchback, one hand resting on the garbage bag of clothes, the other holding the phone in front of my face as I almost yelled down the line, 'I'm going to throw out everything except for one garbage bag and three boxes! That's all that I'm going to keep! Hold me to it!' And then I hung up, turned the ignition and drove to the Brotherhood of St Laurence, singing along with the radio all the way.

I walked into the op shop, head held high, imagining people were looking at me with my big garbage bag and thinking, 'Look at her! She must be very organised to be throwing out that much stuff!' I tried to make eye contact with people, to no avail. 'Probably just jealous of how organised I am,' I thought. 'I'm sure it's not every day someone donates a whole bag of clothes.'

And then as I took a step towards the donation area, the garbage bag broke. It was one of those biodegradable ones. Designed to break down, it had chosen this exact moment to fulfil its destiny. Out spilled my lucky stand-up pants, the T-shirt I had worn my first time on television and some socks I used to wear in high school. I stared at it all in horror. How could I have thought to throw this stuff away? Five seconds ago I had forgotten any of this existed; now I couldn't live without it.

As I was picking everything up off the ground, putting some of it in the donation area and the rest into my handbag, a shop assistant came over. Nobody had seen me come into the shop, they'd only seen me going through stuff and taking it.

'Can I help you?'

I stared up into the face of a middle-aged gent who was frowning down at me, his arms folded across his chest. His offer was made in that tone of voice which indicates no actual help is on offer at all, in fact, nothing is on offer except trouble.

'Oh.' I looked down at my stuff, blinking stupidly, and then back up at him. 'Um . . . it's my stuff . . . I was just . . . it broke . . . I hadn't looked through it you see and I . . . I've just changed my mind on a few things. Like these pants. You probably didn't want them anyway. They're brown. No one wears brown anymore. HAHAHAHA!' I laughed too loudly. He stared at me a moment longer, unsmiling, then stalked off. I kept my head down, shoved the pants, the T-shirt and the socks into my handbag, dropped the rest in the donation bin, then bolted. They had probably decided it was easier to let the mentally unstable lady steal a few things than call the Department of Human Services.

I sat in the car and looked at my bulging handbag. I'd only kept three things, so I'd still ostensibly got rid of a whole bag of stuff. A whole bag! It felt so good that instead of going straight home, I drove to a shopping mall and bought a new dress.

Two days later, Adam called.

'I got your insane voice message. Were you on drugs when you left that? How much more stuff have you chucked?'

'Oh, tonnes!' I was lying. I had tried to throw out a few things from the cupboard in the lounge room, but everything in there was essential: the vacuum cleaner, the brooms, the metre-and-a-half long rendering of Halley's Comet I had made in grade six. Once you took all of that into account, there was barely enough room left for the stuffed animal collection, the torn sleeping bag and the garbage bag full of stamps. I had found fifty-six wire coat hangers though. They were sitting proudly near the door, ready to be donated to some lucky charity.

'Yep, I've been going through the closet in the lounge. I found fifty-six things in there to let go of! And there's another garbage bag full of clothes in the bedroom.'

I didn't tell him I was planning on waiting a year until I had forgotten what was in the bag before I donated it. I also didn't tell him that I'd put that bag inside a second bag, just to make sure there was no repeat of the last incident.

'Well,' said Adam, and he paused for dramatic effect, 'you've inspired me. I'm getting rid of all my shit as well. I've run out of room for my *Doctor Who* tapes and I can't live like this any longer. I'm clearing now, can you hear me? I'm actually throwing stuff into a garbage bag. Hear that?'

I could hear a noise at the other end of the line that definitely sounded like paper crinkling. However, a small part of me wondered whether Adam really was cleaning stuff out of his study, or whether he was just sitting on his couch talking to me while simultaneously rustling a paper bag. It's the kind of thing he would do and then laugh hysterically when I got annoyed with him for lying.

'Tell me I'm doing well. I'm doing well, aren't I?'

Adam is also a hoarder but in a completely different way to me: stuff piles up at Adam's house because he's too shambolic to throw it out; stuff piles up at my house because I become attached to it and start believing it has feelings.

'Yes, Adam, you're doing well. How much have you got rid of?' I hated him.

'Oh, I don't know, this is my second bag full of paper and yesterday I threw out a box of old video tapes.'

'Really?' I put on my best interested voice. 'Wow. How long did it take to go through a whole box of them?'

'Oh, I didn't go through them, I just thought "stuff it, how boring" and I threw them out without looking. Ooooh, hang on, I just found my remote-controlled Dalek!'

I nearly dropped my phone. The idea of throwing something like video tapes out without first sitting down and going through every one of them and then pondering, reminiscing or writing a journal entry about them was anathema to me. He sounded so satisfied. It was awful.

'Adam?'

'Yes, sweet pea? Ooooh! A photo of me! Fabulous!'

'Adam, I haven't thrown anything out.'

'What do you mean you haven't thrown anything out?'

I could hear him in the background, moving stuff around, the garbage bag getting fuller and I knew he'd fill that bag and throw it out without giving it a second glance. This was terrible.

'I've moved stuff around but nothing else has left the house.'

'Nothing? Oh, honey, you're rooted!' And then he laughed and laughed and laughed. You'd think someone had just told him Britney Spears had won the Nobel Prize for Literature. He was gasping for breath.

'You're completely rooted!'

'It's not funny!'

'Oh please. For god's sake, if I can do it anyone can. Lord knows I've got some shit but at least my shit is interesting—Ooh! Another photo of me!—yours is just . . . shit. Get over yourself and throw it out.'

He was right of course. My stuff was shit. When I'd moved in here I'd plied him with alcohol and then forced his champagne-soaked frame up a ladder, heaving those enormous bags full of old clothes all the way to the top of the built-in robes. He'd nearly popped from the exertion. I had stood down the bottom, drinking more champagne and egging him on. He was the only person I knew who not only tolerated my eccentricities but risked a hernia for them.

'Get off the phone and throw something out. Call me later when you've made some progress.'

I hung up, went to the kitchen and made myself a gin and tonic. Then I sat on the couch and watched a rerun of *Touched By an Angel*. When the phone rang a couple of hours later, I almost didn't answer it. If it was Adam, I was going to ignore it; I did not need to hear any more about his brilliant de-hoarding success. However, curiosity got the better of me and in the end I tore my eyes away from the TV, grabbed the phone and looked at the incoming number. It was Thomas. There was going to be a bright spark in this day after all.

'Guess what?' I could hear the smile in his voice.

'What?'

'I just bought a house. I am totally a home owner. We're going to the pub to celebrate. You coming?'

I didn't tell him I was way ahead of him, drinking on my own and watching Roma Downey's character harass a pregnant teenager.

'Sure. Just give me a moment to finish up here and I'll join you soon.'

'Wait!' I just caught his voice before I hit the 'end' button. 'If I'm moving into my own house, that means this flat is empty again. You want it back?'

The room started spinning. He was talking about our old apartment—my dream apartment—with its floor-to-ceiling storage running the entire length of the hallway and its built-in robes in the bedroom. I almost wet myself.

I got off the phone and squealed. All that space! Cupboards! No more meth lab! After two years of living in a hovel that not only looked depressed, but smelt it as well, I couldn't wait to move back into a place where even the floorboards looked happy.

Over the next few weeks I daydreamt about how much happier and organised I would be when I moved back there. My life would start up again. Gone would be this uneasy feeling that something was wrong, that something else was broken and that everything was lost. Gone would be the panic that Adam was beating me in the clearing-out stakes. It all made sense now—the loss of that apartment had been causing my misery. Now I was getting it back. Everything would be okay. I ticked the days off on my calendar.

And I avoided making direct eye contact with my stuff as it sat where it always had, unboxed, unpacked and completely unready to be moved.

Chapter Eight

Four days before moving back into the flat I used to share with Thomas I was panicking. I hadn't packed a thing. There was *absolutely* no way I could pack all of this in time for the removalists. I walked into the kitchen and panicked. I looked at my bookshelves and panicked. I stared at the fifty-six coat hangers still lying next to the front door and panicked. I didn't know what to do. It was ten o'clock in the evening and, like every other night for the past week, I'd come home from work, been overwhelmed by the sheer scale of the job before me, given up on trying and gone to bed. Tonight was going to be no different.

I had just started looking for my pyjamas when the phone rang. It was Thomas.

'Hey.'

'Hey, what's up?'

'Oh . . . nothing.' I didn't want to admit how useless I was.

'Well, I just got burgled. They took all the good stuff and trashed everything else. You don't have to come around, but I've opened a bottle of Jameson's.'

Of course I was coming around. I jumped in my car and drove straight to his house, fretting all the way. He'd only just moved in, it didn't seem fair. Still, this was something that I'd heard happened: people moved into a new place and the boxes out the front tipped off would-be burglars that there might be new stuff inside. Thomas had moved in, plonked the packaging from his new entertainment system out on the nature strip and, two days later, arrived home to discover most of his major appliances and a great number of the smaller ones were missing.

When I got there he was all business, making an inventory of everything that had been stolen. Just as he'd said, the place was completely trashed. The TV and stereo were gone leaving nothing but a few wires hanging out of the walls. His wardrobes had been ransacked and what the thieves hadn't wanted they'd dumped on the floor. They'd even used his suitcases to carry out his clothes. It was the disrespect that upset me the most, and if it had been my house, I would have been a wailing mess. Not Thomas—he was pouring whiskey, and as more friends turned up, he happily took them on a tour of the destruction.

To Thomas, stuff was just stuff. It came, it went and then you spent an enjoyable weekend wandering around appliance stores with your insurance payout replacing it all. As I walked through each room, I remembered when we had lived together and he had shown me all his childhood possessions. They all fitted in one child-sized toy suitcase—that was it. I can remember internally shuddering, not only at the horror of how much he must have thrown away, but at the envy I felt: looking at that case was like watching the devil do a sexy dance. Sure, throwing out my stuff would be like killing my own children, but looking at how little Thomas had kept, it was also deliciously tempting. He seemed so unencumbered.

Around midnight, slightly tipsy from the whiskey, I decided to leave my car where it was and take a taxi. My chin in my hand, I stared out the window the whole way home, watching the darkened houses slip by and pondering how different the pair of us were. Tom was braver than me. Lots braver. Perhaps I would be able to pack my flat if I had him beside me. I thought about it. Was it inappropriate to ask my ex-boyfriend to help me move? No. He'd asked me to come around when he needed help, it was perfectly reasonable for me to do the same. We were friends now, this was what friends did and besides, he was the only person who would know exactly how to fix everything for me. I couldn't ask him right away though, he'd just been robbed, he needed some time to heal. I decided to leave it for a couple of days.

In the end, I left it until the day before I had to move out. I still hadn't packed a thing. I was saucer-eyed by the time I called him.

'Tom, I haven't started. My flat . . . it's . . . I know I should have, but I didn't, I don't know what to do. Could you—'

He offered to help before I even got the words out. I felt my lungs expand for the first time in a week. Then I started to feel like a drama queen. Other people could pack their houses without dragging their ex-boyfriends around to help; why couldn't I? I hadn't rung Adam because I knew that he would have told me to grow up and get on with it. I'd rung Thomas because I knew he'd come. What had I done?

Feeling guilty, I pulled myself together and started the work I should have already finished. By the time Thomas turned up a few hours later, I had managed to pack the bookcases and most of my clothes. I'd also attempted to pack away anything I was too embarrassed for him to see, such as the stuffed-toy collection and two broken computers, the necessity of which I had a feeling he wouldn't understand. I didn't have enough time to get to all of it though. Even if I'd started a month ago, I wouldn't have had time to get to all of it.

When I heard his knock, I ran to the door and opened it nervously. Oddly enough, even though we were spending a lot of time together, this was the first time he had seen where I lived. I had been back to the place we had shared a few times; once he had rung me in a panic to say his trousers were too long and I needed to come around and take them up for him. We had been due at an awards ceremony in less than an hour and I stood at the kitchen bench in my formal frock and full hair and make-up, feverishly hem-ming as he stood in his underwear and watched out the door for the cab to arrive. As he made some joke about me looking like a housewife from the fif-ties, I couldn't help thinking how lucky I was that we were still friends. I also couldn't help thinking how much I wished I still lived somewhere this nice.

Now Thomas was standing in the middle of the mess that was my dank, smelly lounge room, staring wide-eyed and saying, 'Jesus, Mary and Joseph. If they had broken into your place instead of mine, how would you have been able to tell?'

We worked to a system; Thomas assembled the boxes, I chose what would go in each and then he packed it away. We had an enormous amount to get through, preferably before dawn. Ominously, he drew out a garbage bag, fluffed it open, then said casually, 'And this one's for the rubbish.'

A little trickle of sweat ran down my back. I needed Thomas to help me pack, not to throw things out. If the bursting garbage bag of clothes had taught me anything, it was that getting rid of stuff was not a decision that could be made rashly. I had that other bag of clothes waiting to go to charity in a year or so, that was more than enough for now. But from the look of determination on Thomas' face, I had an awful feeling I was going to have to justify some of my belongings. I decided the best plan of action would be to explain each of the things as I handed them over, then he would understand why they couldn't be thrown out. This is what I like to call 'farm logic': you can kill an unnamed chicken for your dinner, but you can't kill a chicken called Betty. Who could? Betty probably had relatives that would miss her. I was going to 'Betty-up' my stuff. I laid my hands on a tattered old book and held it up enthusiastically, grinning like I was the host of a children's show.

'Oh! Would you look at that! This is the first cookbook I bought when I had just moved out of home. It had a recipe for a bean casserole that I cooked nearly every second night because I couldn't figure out how the—'

'Pass it to me so I can pack it, Corinne.'

'Yes, of course. Sorry.' He was right, I couldn't carry on about everything I owned, we would be here all night. Maybe I only needed to Betty-up things that looked really borderline.

'Oh look! This is the cassette-tape holder I made in year nine. I remember my woodwork teacher, Mr Tobin. He was a lovely man, he had a—'

'Corinne, I need to put it in a box.'

'Okay then, you do that.' Jeez. I was just telling a little story that I thought might amuse him. He didn't seem to care at all.

'Hey! Here's the Hello Kitty clock your parents gave me! Remember? I think it was for Christmas, or was it my birthday? No, wait, it might have been—'

'Corinne, you're not reminiscing, you're packing. You can go through it all when you unpack tomorrow.'

Wow. I couldn't believe he didn't want to talk about the clock. I shut up and reminisced to myself instead. Here was the cheese grater that my grandmother used. It was all rusted around the bottom but as long as your tetanus shots were up to date, you could still grate with the top half of it. Oh! Here was the Noddy and Big Ears placemat that I had used every night at dinner when I was a little girl; there was Noddy having a cup of tea with Mr Tubby Bear, while Mr Wobbly Man stood in the foreground talking to Mrs Tubby Bear. Big Ears wasn't in the picture at all. Odd. Why wouldn't you—

'Corinne, you going to pass me that?'

'Sorry. Sure.' I handed it over and started fondling my *Days of Our Lives* coffee mug. Everything held a memory. Everything made me think of something else. The Bettying-up was backfiring.

'This broken bread bin goes in the garbage bag, yes?'

He said it gently but even so, his tone indicated it wasn't really a question. Before I could answer, he threw it out. I was shocked. Could he do that? I supposed he was right—it *was* broken—but it was also a bit waste-ful. A broken bread bin could have been used as a window box for some geraniums. I would need to glue the crack in its side back together, drill some holes in the bottom and maybe see if I could extend it upwards so that it was deep enough to hold plants, but it could be done.

'Umm . . . Thomas? That belonged to my mother.'

'And now it's broken and in the rubbish. Would you like to take it back out and post it to her?'

I couldn't fault his logic, although I really wanted to—I remembered that bread bin from primary school. We always had Sunicrust bread sitting in it and every so often, on rare and beautiful days, Mum would reluc-tantly give in to my and Wendy's pestering and make us jam sandwiches instead of ones with proper ingredients.

'It's just that it reminds me of my childhood.'

'So does every other thing we've packed. How many reminders do you need? You've got the pencils and the pencil cases, all the schoolwork, the school uniforms, the school photos. Unless you are about to tell me that you've got Alzheimer's, surely you can remember your childhood without all of this.'

Maybe, maybe not. It would be too late to know after I'd thrown it all out. We worked on and on. Occasionally Thomas would throw something out and, even more occasionally, I would let it stay in the rubbish. If it wasn't broken, I refused to let it stay there. As the hours passed I could see his jaw tightening and his teeth starting to grind. At around 2 a.m.—as I handed him what appeared to be a baby's bath seat—he lost it.

'What the hell is this?'

I shrugged. 'How should I know?'

'Then why are you keeping it? What the hell is half the stuff I've put in these boxes? Where did all this crap come from, Corinne? I've never seen it before.'

Well no, he hadn't. I'd cleverly hidden it all away in storage when we were living together.

'What the hell are you doing with a baby's bath anyway?'

'Um . . .'

'Well then, I'm chucking it out.'

'No! You can't! It's . . .'

'It's what? You don't even know whose it is! Jesus. Were you auditioning for a role in *The Hand That Rocks the Cradle*? Get rid of it before I start thinking you've lost your mind.'

I sulkily threw it in the garbage bag in the kitchen that was steadily filling with my belongings. Or someone's belongings. I had to admit that the baby's bath seat was confusing, as was the yellow plastic dish drainer that we had found in the bathroom, hidden amongst the towels. I guess I had picked this stuff up from old share-houses when no one else claimed it. I was getting the uneasy feeling that perhaps I might have a few things in my possession that normal people did not. Still, I felt sick throwing them out. What if I remembered their significance tomorrow? Or the next day? It would be too late to retrieve them and they would be gone forever.

'Corinne. What in Christ's name am I holding?'

That's when Thomas found the sticks. The rational part of my brain disappeared.

'Please don't make me throw them out.'

I was crying. These were real tears; I wasn't Bettying-up my stuff now, I simply couldn't bear to part with anything else. I felt utterly pathetic insisting on a photo of those sticks but I couldn't stop myself. That's the problem with addicts: if all it took for us to stop was *knowing* it was wrong, we wouldn't have a problem in the first place. And like a true addict, doing the wrong thing instantly made me feel better. By taking that picture I got what I wanted: I got to avoid regret.

We finished packing around 4 a.m. and Thomas left cranky and exhausted. I only managed to get three hours' sleep before the removalists arrived. It didn't matter to me. I was packed, I had my photo of the sticks, I'd rescued most of my things from the garbage bag and I was going back to the sunshine flat. Everything was going to be okay.

I watched anxiously as every single box was carried out to the van. I irritated the removalists with all my questions: 'Are you sure things won't move around?' 'What if you go over a speed hump?' 'What about if you have to brake suddenly?' 'Or slowly? Will things move then?' 'On second thoughts, I'll take that mirror back out of the truck and put it in my car instead. I wouldn't cope if anything happened to it.' 'Okay. I'll go back inside and check I haven't forgotten anything.' 'Are you sure that I can't— okay, I'm going.'

I drove behind the van the whole way to the new flat, keeping an eye on the back doors just in case one of them unexpectedly flew open.

I started unpacking in the new place as soon as the last removalist walked out the door. I ran around the little lounge room and bedroom like I was on speed. In less than a week there was not a thing out of place— nothing hidden under tables or chairs, nothing piled up on the coffee table or down the side of the fridge. There was even one whole cupboard above the European-style laundry that remained empty. I can remember thinking that the architect wouldn't have included so many cupboards if that wasn't the amount an everyday person needed. Clearly I did not have a problem at all. Never mind that it had taken the removalists nearly the whole day to move me in, never mind that it had cost me nearly one thousand dollars to do it, never mind that Thomas thought that I was certifiably nuts. The packing, the move, the money, it was all worth it because now I was living like a normal person.

And I hadn't had to throw out any of my precious belongings to do it.

Part 3
Where It Collapsed

Chapter Nine

I can't put a finger on the exact date when it fell apart. It probably started the day after I moved in and I didn't notice because I was so busy with the rest of my life. Things must have imperceptibly shifted themselves from the outside world into my house. It wasn't as if I actively went out and gathered possessions—I didn't buy unnecessary clothes or books or knick-knacks—it was just that if something entered my house, it never left again. I wasn't so much a consumer as a hostage taker.

Over time, I got myself into a beautiful rhythm. Adam would come around every Monday night and we would sit on the balcony and gossip until the wine ran out. (The wine bottles were stacked up in the kitchen, waiting to be turned into candle-holders like I'd seen in French cafés.) Thomas, myself and a bunch of friends would catch up every weekend and occasionally we would go away on trips together. (There were photos and souvenirs from these trips somewhere in the flat, I just didn't know where.) I even managed to get myself into a hopeless relationship with a musician that was so tenuous as to almost not exist. (There were letters from him stashed in a drawer, I just wasn't sure which one.) My life had gone on as usual; the stuff must have crept in when I wasn't looking.

The only real change had been to Thomas' love life. He had met a beautiful woman called Sarah and it was obvious this was going to be a long-term thing. I surprised Adam by being thrilled when I heard the news. I didn't want to explain it to him, but the guilt over breaking up with Tom had never left me. It was the most hurt I had ever inflicted on another person, and the look on his face when I had said I was leaving was something I couldn't forget. It was even worse now I was back in our old flat. Often when I closed my eyes at night I could still see him—standing in the kitchen, right between the kitchen bench and the wall heater—his whole body seeming to shrink as he realised that I was really going. Ever since moving back I had not been able to sit on my couch because, if I did, I was staring straight at that spot and the whole awful thing would come back to me. It was the little girl in Waltons magnified to the power of infinity. But now Thomas had Sarah. Maybe my guilt would finally pack its bags and go.

The stuff, however, would not. The whole apartment was a catastrophe. It seemed like it hadn't taken any time at all for the cupboards to fill up (including the one above the laundry) and I had resorted to hiding things on the dining chairs, stacking things against walls and hiding bits and pieces under the couch cushions. I was back at Level Seven and I knew I had to do something about it. So once again, I decided to make a start.

Things did not go to plan.

Every box I pulled out was too hard to deal with, so instead of going through it, I pulled out another one hoping to find that holy grail: the box that held nothing I wanted to keep. All I found were a lot of old memories—and not all of them were good. In one box I found the order of service from every funeral I had ever been to. In another, I found a letter I had written and never sent to some boy who had broken my heart in the early nineties. This was not like the time I had gone through my clothes; these were not the time machines I was hoping to find at all. It was like I had psychologically booby-trapped my own house. I carefully re-folded everything and put it back in the box, ready to be pulled out in another few years to distress me all over again.

I abandoned the box idea and homed in on the paperwork. It had managed to infiltrate the entire flat. Every cupboard was stacked with files and folders and plastic sleeves of god knew what. There was even paperwork in the wardrobe and the linen closet. I'd never kept a diary, I'd just written on whatever piece of blank paper I could lay my hands on at the time. I employed the same method for joke or story ideas, shopping lists, recipes, people's addresses and phone numbers. As a result, I had stacks of scribbled-on envelopes, notepads, post-it notes and paper bags. I even once found half an idea for a play written on a sandwich wrapper. None of this stuff was filed together. It had snuck into every drawer and shelf and was stashed in piles artfully concealed by a sarong. I had created a paper-based diaspora.

I rounded up as much as I could and started sorting through it. It was imperative that I read every note, every script, every list; I might have unknowingly written a Nobel Prize–winning thought on a supermarket docket. There was so much of it that I soon realised I'd be applying for the pension before I finished. I jumbled it together and shoved it under my desk in the space where the office chair was supposed to fit.

I walked back through the hall and into the bedroom. It was full of half-emptied-out boxes and every drawer and cupboard was open. Strewn across the bed were clothes, yet more paperwork, novelty tea towels and what I supposed was one of my wisdom teeth, wrapped in surgical packaging, the blood still adhering to its roots. Even I recognised that was disgusting.

I felt like I was drowning. What I needed was a bit of control. I plonked down in my armchair and started making to-do lists. I made lists of each area that needed cleaning out. Then I made lists of each of those areas broken down into smaller sections. Then I made lists of those lists just in case they weren't in the right order. I slowly started to feel better. I was doing something constructive, I was making *lists*. I was even using a real notepad I had found in the bottom of my wardrobe. It had Mr Men on it. Every now and then I would stop writing and look around my house, smiling proudly at the work I had not yet done. When I had finished writing out everything that needed to be completed—and had grouped and regrouped it all into themes and areas—I allotted estimations of how many hours it would take to do each bit, allowing sufficient time to reminisce, annotate and sit and stare out a window. It came to two years if I didn't sleep. I wanted to scream.

How had I let this happen? This was supposed to be my fresh start—I was supposed to move back into this flat and my life would instantly become brighter. Not only would my stuff no longer be a problem but my career would pick up, my stomach would become flatter and my hair would grow to be smoother and more manageable. I was supposed to move back into this flat and turn into Heidi Klum.

I stormed into the bedroom and threw back the sliding door of the built-in robe. This was why I didn't go through my stuff—because every time I did, something upset me or reminded me of what a failure I was. The first box I tried to shove back into the wardrobe proved unwieldy. I grunted and pushed and flapped at it uselessly, and when that didn't work, I lost my temper and started yelling at it. I finally got it in and threw another one on top. The stack was sitting on a pile of old pillows and was therefore unstable but I was too mad to care. I picked up a third box and, attempting to reverse body-slam it into place, I lost my balance and fell sideways, just stopping myself from falling by grabbing hold of the sliding door. The box wasn't so lucky. It tumbled back out, taking the other two with it and before I could catch them, they knocked over a full-length mirror. Broken glass splashed across the bedroom floor and into the hall.

I stood very still, just in case something else was about to come crashing down. Then I looked at the carnage in front of me. That mirror had been my favourite possession. I had hidden it away in the bedroom specifically so that visitors couldn't accidentally knock it over. It was my greatest fear that something would happen to it and now it had. I could feel my heart start to beat faster. Thomas had given the mirror to me the first Christmas we had spent together. It was an antique, its frame made out of beaten silvery stuff with little tulips carved all around it. I absolutely adored it. It was the one thing I owned that was worth something. And now I had destroyed it. My ears started buzzing and I could feel the sobs sitting in my chest. It didn't feel like I'd lost the mirror; it felt like I'd lost Thomas.

I looked down at the mess at my feet as the first tears started to fall. Then I stopped crying for a second. There was the photograph of Thomas and the sticks. I couldn't deny it any longer. I was a hoarder.

That should have been as bad as things got—except that I also found something else lying amongst the chaos: the Bastard Man's book. I went cold.

Had I really not returned that old man's book? Obviously not, because it was here, lying in a pile of novelty handkerchiefs, magazines, disintegrating paper clips, candle stubs and shards of pointy glass. I had packed up and moved somewhere nice, with sunshine through the windows and white tiles in the bathroom and next-door neighbours who owned a cat and never cooked up amphetamines in their bathtub. I moved out and I left the Bastard Man behind in his dingy, mildewed hovel. Not only did I not return his book, I didn't even say goodbye. Worse than that, I hadn't even honoured my good fortune by treating the place I now lived in with respect. I'd just filled it up with crap like everywhere else I had ever lived. And, I realised, still holding the photo of Thomas and the sticks, if I did throw anything out, I behaved like a lunatic first.

I bent down to pick up the book—trying to avoid looking under the bed where Brenda Dykgraaf was grinning demonically at me from the side of *Le Marchepied's* box—then I picked my way out to the lounge room and sat down in my armchair. I was trying very hard not to cry. I promised the book I would return it to the Bastard Man as soon as possible, just like I would sort out the devastation I had created in my flat, just like I would figure out how to tell Thomas I had broken the mirror.

Then I began to blubber uncontrollably. Snot ran down my face and because I was crying with my mouth hanging open, I dribbled. I had the book in my lap, petting it gently like it was a dying animal. I couldn't believe that I'd let that old man down. I couldn't even call him to tell him I was sorry because I'd lost my address book somewhere in the nest of crap that was my apartment. And I couldn't bring myself to call Thomas and tell him about the mirror because I didn't want to hurt him. Instead, I just sat there with the book in my lap and cried until the tears stopped and all I was doing was hiccupping. Then I made a decision; if I couldn't get forgiveness from the Bastard Man or Thomas, I would get it from my father. I would call him, tell him how bad I felt about *Le Marchepied* and beg for his mercy.

I started dialling Dad's work number, imagining how happy he would be that we were finally acknowledging this awful, silent hurt that had been sitting between us for so long. I could almost hear the joy in his voice as his prodigal daughter finally made good. When he answered the phone, no words came out of my mouth, just a lot more blubbering.

'Mate? Mate, is that you? What's happened? Are you okay?'

'I'm okay, Dad. I'm okay, I just need to tell you some-something.'

'What? What's wrong?'

This wasn't how it was supposed to go. He sounded really worried, like I was about to tell him I'd shot someone.

'Do you remember that exercise stepper you gave me for Christmas when I was about fourteen?'

'No. What? Mate, what's wrong? Tell me what's wrong and then I can help you.'

'I was mean to you. I didn't say thank you and I didn't . . . I didn't . . .'

Now I was doing that awful sobbing thing where the words only half came out. What I had tried to say was, 'I should have said that I loved it, Dad. I should have said you were a good father.' What he had probably heard was, 'I shuh-uh-suh-I-luh-ee-dah-guh . . . guh..guh-faaaathahhhhh.'

There was silence on the other end of the phone.

Then Dad said, 'What?' again.

I pulled myself together, took a deep breath and said, 'I was mean to you, Dad, and I'm sorry.'

Now he was laughing, and not in the way someone laughs when they've heard a good joke but in the way someone laughs when they think the other person has lost their wits.

'I don't remember it at all, mate. I suppose I gave it to you. Why are you worried about it now?' He laughed again. Nervously.

'Because it's under my bed and I know it's there and it reminds me of what a little bitch I was.'

'It must have been over fifteen years ago.' More laughing.

'I just feel guilty. I've been an awful person, Dad, and I feel guilty.'

'Never feel guilty. That's my motto. Never feel guilty.'

'Thanks, Dad.' But I did. About everything.

Months later, I was still finding tiny splinters of glass all over the flat, not just in the bedroom but in the kitchen, the lounge room and underneath my desk. It got into my feet if I walked around barefoot. I found splinters in my elbows and fingertips. The stack of paperwork was still under the desk and piles of stuff, like droppings, were all over the floor of every room. The Bastard Man's book was still sitting on top of the coffee table and *Le Marchepied* was still underneath the bed. And sometimes I found myself sitting on the couch, staring at the space between the kitchen bench and the heater, twisting my hands together and telling the empty air how sorry I was.

Chapter Ten

With me, things always need to reach breaking point before I take action. I hadn't done anything about the mess in my flat for a month, I'd just wandered around the house—yet again—looking at the piles I should have been be getting rid of and wishing I had never opened any of the boxes in the first place. The Bastard Man's book was still sitting on the coffee table and every time I glanced at it a tingle of guilt shot up my spine.

To make matters worse, Melbourne was experiencing one of its hottest summers on record. Day after relentless day the temperature soared close to forty degrees and, as my flat had no insulation, inside was even hotter. The air conditioner was virtually useless, puffing out tepid air with the approximate force of an asthmatic. I strung blankets across the windows to block out the sun, and when that didn't work, I covered them in tin foil. From the outside it looked like a child had tried to turn the flat into a spaceship. For days on end I was barely capable of moving and I only got dressed if I needed to leave the house. Most of the time I spent in my underwear, skulking around the place slack-jawed with a little moustache of sweat on my upper lip. I made sure I avoided mirrors.

As it was too hot to do anything—least of all clean up—I was manoeuvring over and around little mounds of magazines, clothes, books, paperwork and broken what-nots whenever I needed to get somewhere in the flat. The hotter I became, the more those piles started to annoy me. Eventually, after yet another sweaty, sleepless night, things came to a head. Climbing over a mountain of crap in an effort to get to the kitchen, I tripped over a stack of magazines and fell to the floor, smashing the teacup I was holding. That was it.

'Fuck you!'

I was screaming at Bananarama who were staring moodily up at me from the now tea-splattered front cover of a *Smash Hits* magazine, circa 1987.

'You did that on purpose you frickin' piece of frickin' shitty crappy . . .'

And then, because I had ran out of words, I stamped on the magazine. Sara Dallin's black and white crop-top scrunched under my foot. Sara remained unfazed, arms still folded across her chest. This just made me even more angry. So I punched a wall. Then I stomped out of the kitchen and into the bedroom, picked up whatever clothes were nearest and put them on. I was dressed for the first time in two days. As I made my way back towards the lounge room I started picking things up. I didn't put them back in their boxes, however; I took them straight out to the car. To my heat-addled way of thinking, my possessions were trying to kill me. It was time for them to go.

I loaded the car with old bits of electrical equipment, as much of the clothing as I could fit, some jewellery, an old tape recorder and *Le Marchepied #1 Step*! Then I had the brilliant idea of taking the mirror to a glazier to be fixed. I couldn't figure out why I hadn't thought of that before. Glass is just glass, I hadn't damaged the frame. I felt like an idiot for overreacting the way I had. I searched the phone book, found a glazier and hauled the frame out to the boot. I immediately felt more calm. I could see the floor again. I could get to the kitchen. The coffee table was clear. I didn't stop and pat myself on the back, though; I was worried that if I hesitated for even one second, the impetus to get rid of everything would evaporate in the heat and I would simply leave everything in the car.

I called Adam.

'Hello, sweetpea!'

'My stuff just tried to kill me. Do you want to come to the op shop with me?'

'Sure! I'm ready now.'

It's hard to find someone to accompany you on an errand run. No sensible person enjoys watching someone else drop off their dry cleaning or deposit a cheque. Adam is different. He loves being a passenger because it means he has a captive audience. Short of leaping out at the traffic lights, the driver is trapped beside him while he sings Christina Aguilera's entire back catalogue, screams at pedestrians to do something about their hair or moons a bus full of schoolchildren. Still, a small part of me wished he wasn't available so immediately. I had been hoping he would say 'tomorrow' or 'next week' so that I could put the goodbyes off just a little longer. Instead, he'd said 'Give me five minutes to find some pants without holes in the crotch.'

Good. Okay. Good. I was finally doing something . . . good.

Just before I walked out the door, I grabbed the Bastard Man's book. He lived in the same suburb as the glazier. It was unlikely, but with Adam beside me I might just work up the courage to visit him.

I arrived at Adam's house and he greeted me in a pair of velour tracksuit pants and a T-shirt that read: 'I ate all the pies'.

'Today, I am Mariah Carey,' he announced. 'You can be Bette Midler.'

I didn't think he meant it as a compliment to any of us. We got out the street directory to plan the trip. We decided on a big circle heading west, coming back via the op shop and ending up in the east to drop off the mirror before returning home.

Our first port of call was an electrical shop that specialised in the type of battery-operated vacuum cleaner I had owned for years but no longer used because first, the battery needed replacing, and second—now that I lived in a place with floorboards—a vacuum cleaner was redundant. I had tried to palm it off on a number of friends as a sort of permanent loan, but as soon as they found out it didn't work, my offer seemed less generous. Now I was finally going to get it a battery and give it to charity.

It was a twenty-minute drive and along the way Adam interrogated me as to what exactly I was getting rid of today.

'Well,' I said, 'there's the vacuum cleaner, there's a bunch of bags and boxes for the op shop, there's a piece of exercise equipment I've never used, there's the broken mirror to be fixed and there's an old tape recorder.'

'An old tape recorder?' There was an accusatory tone to Adam's voice that made me feel uneasy.

'Yes. A tape recorder.'

'Who wants a tape recorder?'

This was exactly the kind of questioning I had wanted to avoid and was why I had put him in charge of navigation.

'Shhhh. Watch the street signs, Adam. If we miss the turn-off, we'll be stuck all day trying to turn around.'

I was only partly trying to distract him. The battery shop was situated in one of those nightmare shopping strips that not only has a lot of traffic, but also a pedestrian crossing and a train line. If you over-shot it, it might take you the best part of the rest of your life to find a turning point to get back again. Thanks to Adam's map-reading skills, not only did we find the place without difficulty, there was a parking space right outside the front door. I felt a little bit excited; it always augurs well when a day starts off with the perfect park.

We went inside. There wasn't much to the shop, just a bench and a few batteries hanging on the wall behind it. It had that smell about it that workshops get when they are hot, as if the dust was sweating. Behind the bench stood a dour-looking man who was obviously not interested in Adam's suggestive comments regarding possible uses for the larger batteries. He perfunctorily took my vacuum, found the appropriate battery, fitted it and charged me half the price I was expecting.

I understand that in the greater scheme of exciting things that can happen on any given day this would rank fairly low compared with, for example, the love of your life proposing to you, or giving birth, or winning lotto, or finding indisputable proof that aliens live amongst us, but in the day of a hoarder—in the day of someone who has held on to something for years, subconsciously believing they would never part with it, that they would always be a bit hopeless, and that if they did finally let it go, it would either be unfixable or expensive to fix—in the greater scheme of things, something that I had always envisaged ending badly was instead turning out unexpectedly and joyously for the best. We went into the milk bar next door to buy chocolate and celebrate.

And then it started.

'Why are you giving away an old tape recorder?'

Damn, I thought we had moved past this.

'Because someone might want it.'

'Who's going to want an old tape recorder? Why can't I find anything in this shop? Where's the bottled water? Why can't I find the bottled water?'

Adam can get very high-pitched when he is overheated and I worried that the glass in the shopfront might shatter if we didn't get him hydrated quickly.

I shoved a bottle of water into his hand and said, 'Well, it's not really an old tape recorder, it's more of a radio.'

'What?' Water nearly came out his nose.

Now I knew I was in trouble. Even as the words were forming in my head, I knew I could not win this argument.

'The tape recorder doesn't actually work. Neither does the battery compartment. But if you plug it into a power source, you've got a wonderful radio.' I was like Sir Edmund Hillary, struggling up an Everest made entirely of my own spurious arguments.

Adam pursed his lips, paid for his already half-empty bottle of water and walked out of the shop. This was a bad sign. Silence always means an eruption with Adam. He wasn't being quiet because the argument was over, he was conserving his energy so that he could turn into a great big hairy Krakatoa the moment I joined him in the car.

I took a long time paying, fiddling around with bits of change, hoping he would forget the whole thing in the seconds it took me to follow him. I dawdled out of the shop, slid back into the driver's seat and started the ignition, all the while avoiding making eye contact with the seething ball of velour-encased incredulity sitting beside me. It didn't help.

'What do you mean it's a radio? Everything's a radio! My mobile phone is a radio! Your car is a radio!'

'Yes, but this is an old-school radio. Some old bloke might want it for his shed.' I was pleading. I knew how thin my argument was, but it was the only one I had.

'Oh, brilliant idea, Corinne. And then his life is ruined the moment he tries out the tape deck and it chews his favourite Vera Lynn cassette.'

'He'll still be able to listen to the cricket.'

'No one will want it! Throw it out!' He was screeching, flapping the street directory around as if there were invisible bats trying to attack his bald head.

'I can't! It's hard enough letting go as it is, I can't just throw it out, this tape recorder means a lot to me.'

I wasn't lying, it did mean a lot to me. I had won it in a colouring competition when I was ten. We'd had to colour in a picture of a dragon in bed. His large, reptilian body was covered by a quilt and he was holding a lovely cup of tea whilst enjoying the view outside his bedroom window. What made my entry stand out from the others was that I'd used glitter pens, making first prize a virtual *fait accompli* in the pre-adolescent world of colouring competitions. I was so excited when I found out that I'd won that I temporarily let it go to my head. Being ten and not having a great grasp of electronics (a grasp that has continued to elude me to this day) I told everyone that I had won a stereo. My mother kept correcting me patiently, saying, 'A tape recorder, Corinne, you won a tape recorder.' I wasn't deliberately exaggerating, I was just stupid.

'So what you're telling me is that this tape recorder is well over twenty years old.'

'Well, yes.' Damn. This wasn't working out the way it was supposed to. 'I won it when I was ten, so I suppose that's about—'

'Actually, it would be older than that. Everyone knows you never win anything good in colouring competitions, it was probably ten years old when you won it. So that makes it a thirty-four-year-old tape recorder. Perhaps we should take it to a museum instead.'

I wasn't 'everybody' but I had never heard that you only won old stuff in colouring competitions, and even if that was the case, it didn't change anything. I had loved that tape recorder. I'd won it fair and square and it had been beside me for years. It had comforted me with familiar tapes from my childhood and hometown when the distance and the strange-ness of the city overwhelmed me, and towards the end of its life, after Thomas and I had broken up and I had moved into the hellhole, it kept me company in the bathroom when I showered. Although the volume didn't go loud enough to enable it to be heard over the running water, it still felt comforting to have it there. I couldn't just throw it in a bin; it was family.

'You, my friend, are a Hanrahan.'

As far as retorts go, I was quite proud of that one.

Not being as well versed in obscure turn-of-the-century Australian poetry as I was, Adam told me to shut up and stop being a wanker.

I wouldn't have known who Hanrahan was either except that I had a teacher at school whom all the others used to call by that name. The poem was about a farmer called Hanrahan who expects the worst out of every situation. If things are going badly, he sees them going worse. If things are looking good, he can see the bad just around the corner. Adam was being a Hanrahan and I wanted no part of it. Everything was going my way today; why ruin it with all this talk about the tape recorder being a dud and wrecking some imaginary old bloke's life?

We argued all the way to the Brotherhood of St Laurence, which was a half-hour drive. Because of the debacle with the garbage bag last time I'd gone to a Brotherhood, I'd insisted that this time we go to a different store. I was scared that if I went back to the same one, I'd be arrested when I walked in. This gave Adam even more to berate me about.

'Corinne, they won't even remember you!' Adam took a slug from his water bottle and splashed a little on his neck, like it was eau de cologne. 'It won't be the same staff working there anyway,' he continued. 'Everyone knows you only volunteer in a charity shop when you're a hundred and five years old. The bloke that thought you were shoplifting is probably in a nursing home by now.'

I shot him a disapproving look and kept driving.

When we finally arrived, we once again I got a park right out the front. We were so delighted, we actually stopped bickering long enough to marvel at our good fortune. Then we started unloading. Adam carried a box and the vacuum, I carried *Le Marchepied*.

Inside, we dragged our stuff over to the donation bins. The shop was enormous. There were rows and rows of shoes and clothes, there was even a big bin full of socks. There were mannequins modelling outfits and the books were arranged as if in a mini-library. Everything looked cared for and appreciated and I felt like my belongings were going to a good home—better than the home I had provided for them. I carefully placed *Le Marchepied* into the donation bin, gave it a final, loving look, then went back out to the car. This felt good. Someone else would use that stepper now and love it in the way it deserved to be loved.

Adam and I went back and forth to the car four times. On our fifth trip, Adam started fiddling with the passenger door as a signal for me to unlock it. I ignored him and opened the boot, pulling out the only thing still to be taken in. The tape recorder.

'What are you doing?' Adam squealed so high that dogs barked in response.

'Don't. Try. To. Stop. Me.' And off I marched. Adam followed at a distance.

'I'm not going to stop you. If you want to make an idiot of yourself, go ahead. I'll be in the book section.'

I gently placed the tape recorder on top of *Le Marchepied*. This was it, I was actually letting go. I shut the lid on Brenda Dykgraaf's smiling face before I thought too much about what I was doing and instead focused on what a good person I was for donating so much of my life to charity.

Then I went and found Adam. He was in the electrical section.

'Oooh, look at this one, it's got four settings!' He was fiddling with a hair-straightening iron.

I reached out to pick up what looked like a salad spinner but before I could touch it Adam yelled, 'It's an op shop, not a swap meet!' and slapped my wrist.

This, coming from a man who owned the soundtrack to *Doctor Who* on cassette and a wind-up Jesus on wheels. I was just about to retort by asking what, exactly, a bald man was doing looking at a straightening iron, when a kid who looked about nineteen years old got in first.

'You're not going to find much use for that.' He grinned at us both.

He was just making conversation. A normal person would have laughed or rolled their eyes in a 'Huh, aren't I the crazy one?' kind of way. Not Adam.

Adam turned to him and said flirtatiously, 'I've got *some* curly hair.'

Before the guy could fully register what Adam was implying, I grabbed him by the waistband of his tracksuit pants and dragged him out of the shop. Adam sat in the passenger seat and giggled helplessly at himself. I was mortified.

'You could get done for harassment or something, Adam! What were you *thinking*?'

Adam flicked his wrist and said nonchalantly, 'Oh please, in a Brotherhood? No one gets done for harassing young men in an op shop.'

It seemed to me that Adam was confusing charity shops with foreign embassies, but I didn't want to get into yet another argument. I bit my tongue and drove in silence. Adam hummed a show tune, belting out the lyrics when he could remember them.

When we arrived at the glazier's, we yet again got a park exactly opposite the shop on yet another busy road. I wasn't questioning it anymore, this was simply my day. I carried the mirror into the work shed, past sheets of glass leaning against walls. My hands were slippery from the heat and I was so petrified I was going to cause a catastrophe that I walked through the place like I was a UN inspector in a Cambodian minefield. I gently placed the mirror frame in front of the glazier and, before I could say anything, he took one look at it and said, 'Easy job, mate. Come back tomorrow.' Done.

Now I was starting to believe that my name must have popped up on a celestial good-luck roster. Everything was pointing to this being a day when nothing could go wrong. It was probably because of this that I decided I would drop the book off to the Bastard Man.

'Will you come?' I asked Adam. He didn't really have much choice, he was in my car.

We drove the few minutes from where I had left the mirror to the block of flats I used to live in. I drove around the back to the parking area, looking for a space. Apart from the fact that it was full, it looked the same as always. The grass was overgrown, the roof of the parking area was rusting and the poles were bent where we had all run into them over and over again. I could see the back porch of my old flat. The new tenant had put out a pot of geraniums and there were real curtains on the kitchen window. Despite the improvements it still looked depressing.

The Bastard Man's car wasn't in its usual spot. Normally he parked beneath my bedroom window and if that was taken he'd park around the back. He wasn't there either. I was unperturbed. It was my day. His car was probably at the mechanic's.

I drove back around to the front and parked on the street. I sat and stared at the security entrance through the driver's-side window. The door was chocked open, which was weird. That normally only happened when the couple in the third ground-floor flat were being arrested—which had happened three times when I lived there. There were no police in sight today.

'Why do you think the door's chocked open?' I asked Adam.

'Probably because it's chocked open. Jesus. Get out of the car.'

He started walking up the path. At least now I didn't have to worry about using the intercom to get in. That had been one of my biggest fears, that I would call the Bastard Man up on the intercom and he wouldn't remember me or, worse, he would remember me all too well and would start yelling, 'Book bastard!' and throw stuff from his second-floor window down on my head.

We climbed the two flights of stairs and, as we approached his door, I could see that it was open. Now a sense of foreboding started to wheedle its way in. Two more steps and I was in front of the open doorway and everything was wrong. The flat was completely empty, painted white, and the only inhabitant was an electrician standing on a ladder in the entrance way, fitting some wires.

I was still counting on this being my day. There was a chance—a slim one, but still a chance—that everything was all right. Maybe the Bastard Man was in a nursing home or maybe, I fantasised for one foolish moment, he was renovating. As pointless as it seemed, I asked the electrician if he knew what had happened to the old man who had lived in this flat. Maybe the Bastard Man had moved. I could ring around and find him. I could travel interstate. I could hire a private detective.

'Yeah, didn't you hear?'

My god, the electrician did know. And it sounded exciting.

'He shot himself in the head. Right here in the kitchen.'

I blinked. Nothing else, I just blinked. I turned around to see if Adam was still there. He was. He was staring at me. This was utterly wrong. If I was going to be in one of those 'it was just like something out of the movies' moments then it should involve a tropical island, George Clooncy and an inflatable pool pony. It should not involve some middle-aged bloke in a pair of overalls with a burnt patch near the crotch.

I turned to Adam, horrified, and the first words out of my mouth were, 'Why did I leave it so long? Why didn't I come last week?'

The electrician freaked out. 'Oh shit, are you a family member? I'm so sorry. Shit.' He was still standing on top of the ladder.

'No,' Adam said, 'she used to be his neighbour. It's just a bit of a shock for her.' I was too stunned to notice that Adam was behaving like a normal person.

Adam had once told me that men panic when women get teary and that the panic usually leads to them doing something inappropriate. In this case, the electrician offered to show us around the house. I was too shocked to refuse. It was just a white box now, with whitish carpet and whitish blinds and whitish walls. Gone were all the papers piled up to the ceiling, gone were the mildew and the television, my computer desk, the books and the empty bottles. Everything that the Bastard Man owned, everything that was him, had disappeared. A shiver ran through me as I realised that we are all only one trip to the dump away from being obliterated. None of us are permanent.

The electrician said, 'You should have seen the amount of blood on the walls in here.'

I thought, 'Yes, that's a helpful thing to say. That's completely distracted me from the violent death of an old man. Now I feel like having a good laugh and talking about stain removers. Oh, well done, my electrician buddy, you should drop this electrical gig and open up as a grief counsellor.'

Adam dragged me out of the flat before I could kick the fool in his scorched groin. On the way back down the stairs we met each other's eyes and from the look on his face, I knew what he was going to say.

'Don't you dare,' I said.

'You're thinking the same thing.'

'I am not.'

We got back in the car and drove. I stared at the road ahead. I didn't want to look at him. The unsaid thing was hanging in the air and I knew if I looked at him he'd say it out loud. I wanted to pretend it didn't exist. If we kept our mouths shut, we could continue as we were. We didn't have to Hanrahan it.

We got back to his place and I stopped the engine.

'Do you want to come in?' he asked.

I wasn't sure. Part of me wanted the company, the other part of me felt like we had committed a crime and I wanted to get as far away from my accomplice as possible. I said I thought I'd just keep going. He opened the car door and as he turned to get out he said, 'You've got to admit though . . .'

'Don't, Adam.'

'You are never going to let go of that book now.'

I drove off. I felt sick and ashamed and sad and angry. What happens to an old man, a man who has made it into his eighties, who has been to war, who has raised a family, who has lived on his own for years, what happens after all of that to push him too far?

Maybe he had been diagnosed with terminal cancer and decided he didn't want to go through with the treatment. Maybe his emphysema had got so bad they wanted to put him into a nursing home and he didn't want to go. Maybe he'd had a fight with his son. Maybe he'd just got drunk and it was a rash decision. Maybe he looked around him and saw nothing but rotting junk and decided he'd already died anyway. I felt cold inside when I thought about it.

It had been such a good day. It had ended so badly.

Of course I didn't get rid of the book; I couldn't figure out what to do with it. If I could think of something meaningful, then I would have done it, but what's meaningful about an old book? It wasn't important to anyone now except me. He was a lonely old man. Someone had to care that he was gone.

That night I checked the Brotherhood of St Laurence website to see if I could track where the things I'd donated had wound up. It was a stupid idea, I knew that, but I just wanted to feel like I was in control of something. The information wasn't there. The only thing I did find out was something I should have checked before I left home that morning—they didn't accept exercise equipment. Which meant that *Le Marchepied* had been thrown out.

None of us are permanent.

Chapter Eleven

Thomas was angry with me and I didn't know why. I had called to tell him about the Bastard Man but the conversation was not going the way I had expected. In all the years I had known him, he'd never, ever got angry with me when I was upset.

'He was an old man, Corinne, you barely knew him.'

'I know that, Tom, but it was my worst fear that he would be dead. And he was. Is. It's . . . I don't know . . . I can't help thinking it was my fault.'

I heard him sigh.

'Hey, I got your mirror repaired. You know the one you gave me? I broke it, but I got new glass put in it. You can't even tell anything happened.'

I had no idea why I was telling him this. Was I trying to unburden myself?

'Okay, so you got it repaired.' He sighed again. 'It's just a mirror.'

'I can't repair what I did to the Bastard Man though.'

My voice sounded tiny. His came back at me at full volume.

'Well, I can't help you with that, can I? I can't fix everything for you.'

I pulled the phone away from my ear and looked at it incredulously. What was going on? Thomas liked fixing things, that was what he did. If he didn't, then why did he offer all the time? I started to feel a little indignant. It wasn't as if I didn't pay him back; I was always there when he needed me. Wasn't I? Well, apart from the time I'd dumped him, but that was different. The rest of the time I was there for him; I listened when he needed to talk, I kept him company when he was worried, I helped him in his garden, cleaned up after his parties, I'd even gone to a family funeral with him. Our friendship had never been a one-way deal.

'Corinne, I'm busy, okay? You're going to have to deal with this yourself for a change.'

Stung, I hung up the phone. For a while now he had sounded irritated whenever I spoke to him. What was up with him? If I had done something wrong, I needed to know what it was. I cleared a pile of paperwork off my computer, sat down at my desk and wrote him an email. I told him that he was hurting me, that he was being childish and that I deserved better treatment. As I wrote, the email got angrier and angrier. I ended it by telling him that I deserved a hell of a lot more respect than he was currently showing me. Then, without even bothering to reread it, I sent it.

An hour later, I wished I hadn't. My mother had always told me, 'Never send a letter when you are upset.' She was right, and now that I had calmed down, the situation didn't seem so bad. Maybe Thomas wasn't angry with me at all, maybe he was just busy and I'd called him at a bad time. I inwardly cringed at what I'd written. I pulled the email back up and reread it. Yep. I really should have sat on it. I sounded strident and adolescent and if there was a way to make an email sound high-pitched, I'd found it. Any moment now Thomas would write back telling me to stop being such a drama queen. Or worse, he'd ring me and tell me to grow up. I promised myself I would show emotional restraint from here on in.

I was just about to call and apologise when he wrote back. His email was cold. It was worse than cold, it was furious and dispassionate, like he was writing to someone he barely knew. He called me 'awful and offensive'. I was so shocked that I recoiled from the words on the computer screen. I loved Thomas, there was no way I would ever do anything to hurt him. My resolve to act like an adult disappeared. I rang him and burst into tears.

'Tom, I didn't mean to hurt you, I was just upset. You know how much I care about you, you know I would never intentionally do anything to harm you.'

I had been beating myself up over the Bastard Man, I already felt like the lowest, most evil person in the world, I couldn't bear the idea of Tom hating me as well.

'You know what? I don't care what your intention was, you insulted me—you insulted me completely.'

What had I done? A part of me realised he was overreacting but I was so busy overreacting myself that I couldn't get a grip on the situation. So I just apologised, over and over again. I didn't know what else to do. The idea of losing Thomas' friendship was unbearable. The dorky little kid from Corryong who wore clown jumpers, fell down escalators and was terrified of city people was essentially who I still was. The world scared me, Thomas knew that. In fact, he was the only person who knew that. Adam was my best friend but Thomas was more. Thomas was the only person who really knew that I was hopeless at getting by on my own. If it wasn't for him, I would have floated off into space long ago. I pleaded with him to believe that I was sorry, that I didn't mean to hurt him, that I loved him and cared about him and that I needed him to know that. Eventually he said that he believed me. But he still sounded cold.

I hung up the phone, put my head in my hands and tried to calm down.

I didn't know what to do after that. For weeks I was so scared that I might offend him again that I stopped asking him direct questions and instead became thoroughly and horribly passive-aggressive. Instead of asking if he was going to a friend's wedding, I asked what he was doing that weekend. Instead of asking if he could help me with my budget, I mentioned that I was having trouble using the template he had made for me.

And instead of asking if our gang was still going on our annual holiday together, I asked if he was taking his holidays at the same time as usual. I was behaving like such a martyr that I started to irritate myself.

'Corinne, if you're trying to ask me what I'm doing for New Year then just come out and say it.'

'Sorry. It's just that we hadn't discussed it and I didn't know . . .'

'Well you know now, okay? We're not going away this year. Sarah wants to visit her parents in Mildura, so we're going there instead. If you wanted to know if I was organising a trip, you should have just asked. This implication that I am somehow dishonest is really offensive.'

'No! That's not what I meant! Thomas, everything I say to you is wrong now. I don't know how to fix this.'

This had to be a bad dream, it just had to be. I was losing him and I didn't know how to stop it. I could hear the anger in his voice.

'So this is my fault, is it? Now you're saying that I'm being awful to *you*? Why don't you stop and think about how you sound when you talk to other people?'

He hung up. I felt like dirt. I sat down on the couch and tried to stop shaking. Thomas thought I was a total bitch and I couldn't convince him otherwise. The idea sickened me. I went back over the last couple of months, trying to figure out how I could change things, how I could make him calm down, how I could prove to him that I was the same person I'd always been. I started to panic when I couldn't come up with a solution.

A week later, I received a group email from him announcing that he and Sarah were engaged and that the wedding invitations would be sent out in due course.

I laughed out loud when I read it. If I had been a cartoon character, I would have slapped myself on the forehead and yelled, 'Duh!' Now everything made sense. Thomas wasn't angry, he was stressed. He'd probably been so nervous about proposing that he had taken it out on me. In fact, he'd probably been like this with everyone and I was being paranoid and a little bit egotistical to take it so personally. Thomas was getting married and, like the email said, I was going to be there to help him celebrate. I felt like I could breathe again.

A few days later I saw him at a friend's birthday party. When the bar closed, he invited everyone back to his house, making a point of asking me too. My theory had proven correct, we were back to normal. Tom and I ended up in the kitchen, talking for hours in the old familiar way we always had.

'You going up to The Wrong for Christmas?'

Thomas had nicknamed Corryong 'the Wrong' after I had killed the turtle. I laughed.

'No, we're spending it in Albury–Wodonga with the cousins.'

'Ooooh! Fancy city folk!'

I laughed again and punched him in the arm. I couldn't believe it. It was as if nothing had ever happened. I had lain in bed awake countless nights, trying to figure out how I could win back Thomas' friendship and I hadn't been able to come up with anything. The rest of my time was spent desperately trying not to think about how I would cope without him. Now, incredibly, it was all over. There was no point in bringing any of it up, I was just so glad to have my friend back that nothing else mattered. I left the party as the birds were starting to sing, and as I walked home, I cried with joy. My life was back to normal. Everything was OK.

Two weeks later the wedding invitations were sent out. I wasn't invited.

Chapter Twelve

I was in Sydney, staying with my old friend Jamie when I found out. He owned a house with a pool and he, his girlfriend Emily and I had made the most of the last few days of summer, slobbing around the decking, dipping our toes in the water and generally avoiding the things we were supposed to be doing. I had work to do but sitting by the pool drinking beer and eating pizza seemed like much more fun.

I looked over at Jamie: he was still far cooler than I was. He was wearing aviator sunglasses, he had some kind of weird, patchy multicoloured thing going on in his hair and his girlfriend looked like she belonged in a rock band. I was wearing a one-piece swimsuit I'd been given as a twenty-first birthday present. It was hard to believe either of them was willing to be seen in public with me. I smiled, overcome with affection for them both.

'Remember when I stayed at your place in Bondi?'

I was being sentimental, reminiscing about a time nearly ten years earlier.

Jamie looked at me quizzically.

'No. How long were you there for?'

'Nine days! You don't remember? Wow, Jamie, maybe lay off the beers.'

'Are you sure?'

I started at him disbelievingly.

'Yes I'm sure! I remember us both sitting on the floor in front of your little bar fridge with my hair dryer, trying to melt out a bottle of vodka that had got trapped in the ice in your freezer. You don't remember that?'

He stared at me blankly. I took a swig of my beer and as I did, I remembered that I hadn't actually done that with Jamie, I'd done it with Adam when we were staying at Jamie's place and Jamie was out of town. In effect, we'd stolen his vodka and I was just now, ten years later, incriminating myself. I sneaked a look at J. He look perturbed. I decided it was better to let him think he was suffering from alcohol-induced memory loss than to own up to my crime.

Emily got up from the pool deck, picked up the pizza boxes and wandered back into the house. On the way she called over her shoulder, 'Oh, hey, are you going to Thomas' wedding?'

The world, just for a millisecond, swerved off its axis then righted itself again, like I was experiencing a little bit of psychological vertigo. Nope. I hadn't heard that right. She must have said 'engagement party'. That would make sense. I'd been in Sydney for a week, the invitation was probably sitting in my letterbox at home.

Jamie jumped in quickly, saying, 'You won't be here, Corinne. It's when you're in Perth for that gala show.'

There was no vertigo this time; instead, everything spun rapidly. Thomas was getting married and I wasn't invited. Being out of town didn't make it okay, in fact it made it worse.

'Jamie, you're invited and you'll be in Perth too.' I said it in the calmest tone I could manage. I shook my head, smiled casually at Jamie and slipped into the pool. I just needed a moment underwater where no one could see my face.

I felt so betrayed. Tom and I had spent hours talking at that party like everything was fine. Why hadn't he told me then? Why had he decided to let me find out from someone else? There was absolutely no way that he couldn't have known how much this would hurt me. After years of being best friends, years of parties and funerals and cups of tea and glasses of wine and stupid jokes and tears on shoulders, he was ending it all in the cruellest way possible. He was about to celebrate the biggest day of his life and he didn't want me there.

I got out of the pool and walked into the house, trying hard to look indifferent. I went to the bathroom and showered. I shut my brain down. We were all going out that night and I couldn't afford to fall apart. I turned the shower off, dried my hair and put on my make-up, staring at my face in the mirror like it belonged to someone else. I wasn't capable of looking into my own eyes. I froze a smile on my face, went back out to the deck and grabbed another beer. I chatted non-stop with Emily while Jamie got ready. If I was left alone with my own thoughts for even a second, I knew I would crash. I talked at Emily and then, when Jamie came out and Emily went to use the shower, I talked at him. God knows what I was saying, I just needed words to come out of my mouth.

We ordered a taxi, we went to the club, we watched the band and I stood there and smiled and laughed and acted like nothing was wrong.

That night I lay in the dark in Jamie's spare room, staring at the ceiling. I wasn't even crying, the tears simply leaked out of their own accord. Thomas had so much contempt for me that he didn't care how much he hurt me. That was the only conclusion I could draw. The realisation made me curl in on myself like a wounded animal. There were so many people who had a reason to be angry with me: my father, the Bastard Man, the little girl in Waltons, the turtle I had murdered. All of them would have been justified in seeking their revenge. But Thomas? He must have simply woken up one day and decided I was worthless.

I left Jamie's house the next morning, smiling and waving like nothing was wrong. I took a cab to the airport, I flew back to Melbourne, I took another cab home and then I walked into my apartment, looked around and fell apart. I wanted to burn the place to the ground. Everything reminded me of Thomas. Here was the newly repaired antique mirror, the kitchen utensils, the framed vintage poster, the clothes, the books, the bowls and jewellery boxes and bottles of wine. I had held on to all of it because it made me feel secure, like I existed, like I mattered, like I had a place in the world. None of it was enough. None of it could make up for what I had lost.

I looked again at everything Thomas had given me, most of it after we'd broken up. The vintage poster stood out from everything else. Something started itching at the back of my brain. He had given it to me about a year after I'd left him. He had dragged it all the way back from some Eastern European country and then had it professionally mounted. Most people brought back tea towels or key-rings from their holidays, they didn't bring back artwork and have it custom framed for their ex-girlfriend.

I dropped my bags and sat down on the floor, right where I was. How had I not seen this before? Maybe all of those gifts had been his way of trying to win me back. How could I have been so stupid? I should never have taken that poster from him, I should have kissed him on the forehead, told him he was wonderful and then told him to give it to someone else. But I didn't, I took it from him. I'd taken and taken and taken and now, all these years later, he'd realised how selfish and self-absorbed I was and he hated me for it.

I curled up in the space between the kitchen bench and the wall heater, right where Thomas had been standing when I had told him I was leaving. I wanted to stay there forever. I wanted to lie still and small and useless. I couldn't harm anyone else if I didn't do anything. I shifted my right hand and, as I did so, I felt something sharp dig into it. I turned it over. There was a little sliver of glass poking out of the heel of my palm. The broken mirror was still making its presence felt. If I was right, if Thomas had tried to win me back, then I was a stone-cold bitch for not seeing it, and now that he had Sarah, he could see that as well. Sarah was no doubt decent and considerate. She probably didn't live in a house filled with dead flowers and all her socks from primary school. And she could probably look after herself and didn't need Thomas to do it for her. No wonder he didn't want anything to do with me; I was nothing but a leftover from a life that didn't matter anymore.

I pulled the splinter of glass out of my hand, dropped it back on the floor and stared at it. There were probably a hundred more shards just like it still scattered throughout the house. I'd never be able to get rid of them. I guessed that was the same way Thomas felt about me. I flicked the bit of glass so that it fell between a crack in the floorboards. Now I could see things from Thomas' perspective and that hurt more than everything else put together. I dug the splinter of broken glass back out of the floorboards and pushed my palm down on top of it again. Broken things never really leave you. You have to leave them.

Part 4
Where It Was Rebuilt

Chapter Thirteen

I woke up just as the plane was landing. I stumbled to my feet, straightened myself up as much as possible and disembarked. I collected my luggage and slowly, carefully staggered my way into another country. I was walking through Denpasar airport like I was walking underwater, on my way to a yoga retreat in Ubud. And I was drunk. I found my driver and grinned at him lopsidedly. Just two weeks before, I had been lying on Adam's couch crying over Thomas.

'Are you sure this is all you're upset about? I know you were close, but you just seem really, really upset.' Adam was stroking my hair as I lay in his lap. I was sniffling and wiping my nose on my sleeve. I hesitated before answering him. I didn't want to tell him the whole truth. I didn't want to confess that I deserved to be hated by Thomas.

'Of course I'm really upset, Adam. How would you feel if I told you that I hated you? I thought the world of Thomas and now it turns out that . . . I don't know. It hurts. I feel like . . . there's no words for it . . . I think it's . . . it's . . .'

'Life.'

Adam was staring down at me with a businesslike look on his face.

'It's life, Corinne. Shit happens and you get hurt. It happens to everyone. You're not going to be able to find the words for it because it's

123

too universal for that. Ooooh!' He looked delighted with himself. 'I sound like Dr Phil! Might I suggest that you don't spend the rest of your life wallowing in self-pity?'

'Dr Phil doesn't speak like that, Adam.'

'Well he should. I'm sorry, sweetpea, it's just that I can't stand you being this miserable. Maybe you should go to Bali.'

I wrinkled my nose. What a hideous 'woman in her thirties trying to find herself' cliché. Next he would be telling me to enrol in an adult education course in leadlighting.

'Go to a yoga retreat. Sit somewhere warm and meditate.'

'Does it have to be Bali?'

'Stop being such a snob. It's very un-Australian not to like Bali.'

'Have you been?'

'Lord no! That place is for bogans.'

A yoga retreat did sound appealing, if for no other reason than I would fit in better at a place like that than at a glamorous health resort. Those posh places were full of models and people who had paid surgeons a lot of money to make them look like models; they probably did nothing but drink vegetable juices, meditate and have daily colonic irrigations. I wanted to go somewhere where I could wear tracksuit pants and stretch a bit; I didn't want someone shoving a hose up my yoo-hoo. And I wanted— needed—somewhere gentle. Perhaps Bali was the right place for me.

Now that I had arrived, in the wee hours of the morning with a bottle of wine still sloshing around my brain, it felt bizarre. From the bubble of the four-wheel drive all I could see were the lights of the shop signs, all written in English: furniture shops, clothing shops, McDonald's, McDonald's, McDonald's. I could have been anywhere in the world, except that here it was hot and humid and smelt just slightly greener, even at one o'clock in the morning.

We got to the retreat and I carefully followed a staff member up and down a confusing number of steps and paths to my room. I smiled politely and said, 'Thank you' in the careful, over-enunciated speech of the smashed. Then I dropped my bags, pulled a Bintang out of the mini-bar and went back outside to sit on the balcony. My room was enormous, and because of the way the retreat had been designed, I couldn't see any other buildings. I was completely alone and looking out into blackness. I had no idea what was in front of me or behind me or beside me, and all I could hear was the scurrying of a (hopefully) non-venomous animal in the foliage. I watched a gecko crawl along the railing until he leapt off into invisibility. I drank my beer and collapsed into bed. Tomorrow would be better. Tomorrow, I would be on holidays. I was glad I had drunk the extra beer; my brain was now too sluggish to think about how pathetic I was.

The next morning I woke early. I had forgotten to close the curtains and the sun was now sliding across my half-opened eyes. Surprisingly, I wasn't annoyed. No matter what state I was in, I was still on holidays and the little things that would have annoyed me at home (like waking up at 5.30 a.m. with a hangover) now seemed exciting. I was lying on my side, looking out through a wall full of windows at terraced rice paddies, speck-led here and there with coconut trees and tiny figures ambling amongst them. I hadn't seen any of this last night. It was ridiculously idyllic and I couldn't help laughing. I was an idiot to have thought I didn't want to come to Bali. Who wouldn't want to wake up to this every day? Maybe I should move here permanently. I could leave Thomas and my house full of stuff behind and start again. With a warm breeze coming through the windows and the palm trees swaying against the cloud-covered sky, he already felt too far away to worry about.

I wandered down a different set of steps from last night, following the sound of a gong, to the first yoga class. I passed fresh offerings of flowers and rice laid at the feet of the stone gods that were placed in niches and on plinths at regular intervals. All the pebbled paths were scrubbed clean

and somewhere below a stream gurgled. The retreat was carved into the
side of a mountain and designed in such a way that you could only ever
see tiny portions of it at a time. Everything smelt of water and earth and
frangipani and I could hear the swish of the palm trees like gentle rain.
Even the air, with its comforting wet warmth, felt easier to breathe than
the air back home.

The yoga class was conducted on a platform built high above the
stream, with palm trees and tropical flowers surrounding it. A rattan roof
spread above us and at the front sat our instructor, Adi, leading everyone
in meditation. I awkwardly shuffled past twelve other women who were
sitting cross-legged with their eyes closed. I grabbed a mat and settled
down on the far side of the pavilion. I didn't close my eyes like the others;
instead I looked around at my classmates. Some of the women were my
age, a few were older, and there was one lady who looked to be about
eighty. She was sitting on a chair instead of the floor. And she was wearing her nightie. A woman on the other side of the pavilion with long black
curly hair opened her eyes and met my gaze. She grinned broadly and
winked at me. She looked like fun. I took a deep breath and tried to focus
on being in the moment.

The yoga was challenging. I was not as adept as I had expected to be.
I couldn't keep my balance when everyone else could. My Tree Pose was
a joke and even basic poses like The Warrior—where all I had to do was
stand still in a half-lunge with my arms at shoulder height—proved impossible. What the hell was wrong with me? Even the elderly lady (whom I
later discovered was called Vy) was doing a better job than me. Of course,
because her hearing-aid was on the blink she couldn't hear Adi's instructions, so she was doing a lot of improvising but, still, she was on her feet
and I was sprawled on the floor.

The more I fell over, the more annoyed I became with myself. I dis-
regarded Adi's mantra of 'Do no violence, especially to yourself' and

focused instead on hating my stupid hamstrings for being so unrespon-
sive. How was I supposed to find my 'truth' if I spent most of my time
flailing around and knocking over other people? I had already poked one
woman in the eye with my right hand and used the rear end of another as
a sort of bounce-board to keep myself upright. I had envisaged meeting
people politely over breakfast, not by head-butting them in the arse.

That afternoon we went for a walk past the rice paddies and up into the
mountains. I stayed at the back of the group where I would do the least
damage. The woman who had winked at me turned out to be a Texan
called Lucy. She was striding purposefully at the front of the pack and she
was fabulous. She wore an enormous sunhat and her deep brown eyes were
permanently crinkled with either joy or mischievousness. She was chatting
away, making friends and asking questions.

'Adi, what do you call that?' Lucy was pointing at a plant.

'*Bunga merah*,' Adi replied.

'And this one?'

'It's called *bungan soka*. The women use it in their offerings.' Adi was
swishing through the grass, squinting up at the sun and shooing away the
stray dogs that crept towards us.

'What about that, what would you call that?' Lucy was pointing at a
butterfly.

'Brian.' Adi started giggling helplessly.

That night there was to be more yoga (which would give me a few
more opportunities to fall over), and after that, we were to go to a Balinese
temple to take part in a cleansing ritual. It sounded like just the kind
of thing I needed—until Adi mentioned we would have to walk into a
pool of freezing water fully clothed. I didn't want to get wet. With all the
associated palaver of taking extra clothes and getting changed in the back
of a minibus, the spiritual aspect of the trip lost its allure. I was feeling
too fragile for all of that. I was relieved when he said that menstruating

women were not allowed to take part. Technically I wasn't menstruating but I convinced myself that I was close enough that it would be culturally insensitive for me to join in.

Two other women—one of whom was Lucy—were in the same position as myself. We all decided to go to the temple anyway, as immediately after the cleansing ritual we were to start a thirty-six-hour silence challenge. This would be our last opportunity to speak to each other for a day and a half. 'See?' I thought. 'I can look like I'm a joiner without having to actually do anything.' I felt like I was back at high school, getting out of Phys. Ed. by rattling a tampon box.

The drive to the temple took an hour, winding up a mountainside in the darkness. We were in a convoy of three vehicles. In my four-wheel drive there were six of us. The driver and his wife sat up the front and murmured to each other in Balinese. We sat in the back, listening to the comforting sounds of their quiet domesticity, not understanding a word of it. Occasionally we would pass a brightly lit shop with nothing inside but a couple of plastic garden chairs and a TV. We passed a local night market where trailers, vans and stalls were packed in tightly next to each other, their sides thrown open to display all kinds of different foods, none of which I recognised. Roadside shops that sold a mumble-jumble of things and advertised public telephones and internet access sat in the middle of nowhere. Then we were in darkness, apart from the occasional house light. I've always liked driving in the dark. Seeing the lights in the distance that signal other people's homes, I imagine the inhabitants are loved, happy and warm inside. Perhaps it really was like that in Bali. The couple in the front almost made me believe it was possible.

We pulled into a car park, empty at this time of night, which butted up against an outdoor ceremonial pavilion, with giant pillars stretching from its giant cement floor to its giant cement ceiling. It looked even more enormous in the dark, with stray dogs growling in its depths, only discernible by the shine of their eyes. Ahead of us the temple complex glowed dimly and to our right a larger ridge swept up into blackness. Just beside the gate leading into the sacred area was an oversized sign that read: 'Attention. It is prohibited to enter if you are during your period.' And after that was added 'For the ladies'. Were there really men who thought that sign was for them? Perhaps the Balinese thought us Westerners were a bit on the stupid side. I thought of all the footage I had seen of drunken Australians on Kuta beach and understood their point of view.

Everyone else went ahead and Lucy, myself and a stunning Dutch woman called Dael stood behind a locked wrought-iron gate and watched as the rest of our group went through the prayers and offerings of the purification ritual. They were sitting on a stone terrace, hundreds of years old, with their hands clasped in the prayer position in front of their foreheads. The spring in front of them was hemmed in by more stone. Ornate carvings ran along its far edge, serving as fountains from which the water poured. Vy was in there with everyone else but had sensibly realised her knees wouldn't hold up to all the dunking in the pond. I watched her gently amused face as the others squealed when they walked into the pool and the cold water rushed over their heads.

Our little gang were not the only people in the temple; local men wandered through the sacred site, smoking and butting out their cigarettes on the ancient stones beneath their feet, and dogs roamed around them, howling and biting each other. Us three and our unholy lady bits sat outside and watched through the bars of the gate.

As the ritual went on I was distracted by a noise behind me. I turned to see a skinny white dog chasing down an equally skinny ginger dog. Eventually the white one caught his companion and, without even offering to buy her dinner first, launched himself upon her and started doing what dogs do best. I shrugged. As long as they were distracted by their own business they weren't biting chunks out of me. Still, I couldn't help thinking that dog-rooting slightly detracted from the spirituality of the place.

After the ritual in the water was finished, the group walked into another part of the temple and we lost sight of them. Not wanting to tire herself out, Vy came and joined us. She stopped short and looked past me into the dark.

'What's going on there?' she asked, confused.

I turned around. The dogs were stuck together. The white one, rolling his eyes and appearing to grit his teeth, was trying to pull himself free of the lady dog and then, as we watched, he turned himself in a sort of yelping half-rotation until he was facing away from his companion. Their rear ends were now joined together by the most delicate of links. They were like a filthy Scotch Finger biscuit. The bitch had a look on her face as if to say, 'Well, this is what happens when you don't ask first. I'll let you go when you've learnt your lesson.' Somewhere in the distance we could hear chanting.

I had nothing better to do, so I took a few photos of the dogs. Then, as they tried to hobble off together, I thought I might film a little of it. Then I stopped. I was at a Balinese temple witnessing a ritual so strict that menstruating women were not allowed to participate. It was probably not appropriate to be shooting dog porn.

'What are they doing?' It was Vy, still peering curiously at the two dogs in the shadows in front of us.

'They're stuck together.' It was a stupid answer but I didn't want to go into detail.

'How?'

I really didn't want to explain this. Vy, with her little round face and flowery kaftan, looked like she came from a world filled with gingerbread houses where sex did not exist, let alone between dogs.

'You know, Vy, they're stuck like two people with piercings get stuck.' That was Lucy, the helpful Texan. Both she and Dael were laughing.

'Piercings? What are they piercing?'

I felt like we were taking Vy's innocence. She was obviously far more genteel than us, and if she had lived this long without knowledge of fetishism and barnyard copulation, then it was probably fair to say she could do without finding out now. But she kept asking questions and, having no other choice, we gave answers (Lucy's more detailed than mine) until Vy not only had a clear understanding of what was going on in front of us, but of all the various parts of the body that young people pierced and the dangers of heavy petting if both parties had bits of metal poking out of the same general area. Then, with nothing left to say, the four of us silently watched the stuck dogs limp around the concrete together as we waited for the others to finish saying their prayers.

When it was all over we gathered together once more and made our way back towards the car park. As we walked, Vy suddenly let out a little gasp and said, 'You know what the worst bit about this is?'

Oh dear. Poor Vy. She patted me on the arm.

'I don't know how to call back to Australia on these Balinese telephones.' She grabbed hold of the door handle of the waiting vehicle and puffed a bit as she pulled herself up. 'So I can't tell my husband what you girls told me until I get home.' She shuffled over to make room for the rest of us. 'Maybe I should get something pierced while I'm here and surprise him.' And she grinned like an imp as we closed the car doors and started our silence challenge.

I stared out the car window all the way back to the retreat, smiling to myself. I hoped I grew up to be like Vy.

I woke up the next morning feeling edgy. Today wasn't just about us not talking—we were not even allowed to listen to music or read. Instead, we were to focus on our inner selves and write down anything pertinent. It was going to be a long time on my own, and considering that my thoughts and I were not getting along at the moment, I reckoned it was probably going to feel a lot longer for me than for anyone else. I wished now that I hadn't welshed on the temple ritual. It might have helped clear out the rubbish in my head. I was so wrapped up in hurt, anger, regret and guilt that I was like a pass-the-parcel no one wanted to be holding when the music stopped.

On my desk sat a notepad and a watercolour set. I picked up the notepad and started writing. I didn't think about it, I just let my thoughts come out uncensored. I was hoping to pour my subconscious onto the page to see if I could make sense of it from a distance. I wrote for an hour without stopping and then went back and read it over.

It started off as anger at Thomas for hurting me. I frowned. I had thought I was feeling guilty but judging by the language on this page, I wasn't so much filled with contrition as I was a potty-mouthed ball of fury. Then gradually, predictably, my anger turned to self-flagellation. Now I was reading that I deserved to be hurt because I had left him. In fact, I deserved this hurt for all the pain and distress I had caused every person I had ever met in my entire life: the Bastard Man, my dad, my sister, the turtle, the little girl in Waltons, Craig in the caravan, Shane Doltrey, the driver who picked me up at Denpasar airport and had to endure me when I was drunk. Then I circled back to Thomas again and another couple of pages were filled with a list of regrets, steadily becoming more and more ridiculous: I had probably hurt Thomas every time I had nagged him to make me a cup of tea; I had probably caused him undue stress by not doing my share of the washing-up; I had probably breathed in the wrong direction on a summer's day in 2004, making a butterfly flap its wings in Sydney, causing a tornado in Paraguay. Of course Thomas hated me and wanted me out of his life: I was a mean, horrible, selfish person. After that I had written a lot of apologies to him and promised to find a way to make up for everything. It finished with: 'When he's happy, I'll be happy.'

I dropped the notepad and stared with disbelief at what was in front of me. Did I really believe that I was responsible for his happiness? Here I was in this tropical paradise to learn how to let go of my own pain and I was wasting my time trying to figure out how I could make him let go of his. And if I stopped beating myself up for a second and really thought about it, I had no idea why Thomas had ended our friendship in the first place; I was only guessing that it was because I'd done something terrible. I chewed my bottom lip worriedly. It said a hell of a lot about me that all of my assumptions started with the belief that I was an awful person.

I stared out the window at the rice paddies. I was trying to control things over which I had no power. No wonder I was such a mess: I had a list of regrets and miseries in my head and I spent every spare moment cataloguing them, reliving them and finding ways to hurt myself with them. I wasn't helping the people I believed I had damaged; I was damaging myself. I looked again at what I had written: 'When he's happy, I'll be happy.' I picked up my pen and scribbled it out. I wasn't in control of Thomas. The only person I could control was myself.

I made a decision: because I would probably never know the real reason Thomas had ended things, the only thing I could do was let go. More to the point, the only thing I could do was let *him* go. Finally, here on a little island in the middle of the Indian Ocean, I got it. This was the 'life' that Adam was talking about. Shit happens. It's how you deal with it that counts.

There was a pile of small squares of paper left in a corner of the writing desk. These were for a ritual that we were to perform on our final day. We were to write on each piece of paper one negative aspect of our lives that we wanted to free ourselves from, and on the final day, we were going to burn them. We could use as many of the pieces of paper as we liked. I used all of them, and when I ran out, I chopped up more to the same size and used those as well.

I wrote 'guilt', I wrote 'regret', I wrote '*Le Marchepied*'. It was like the

133

earth had spun around and shown me the world that everyone—apart from myself—was living in. My father had forgiven me for *Le Marchepied*, why was I not forgiving myself? The little girl in Waltons department store had probably never thought of me again—and if by some slim chance she had, then she was even weirder than me. The Bastard Man was dead. I should be honouring his memory with more than guilt. I wrote 'helplessness' and 'self-loathing' and 'grief'. I wrote 'Thomas'. I wrote until every spare scrap of paper I could find had a word on it. When I was finished there was a pile of twenty pieces of paper in front of me, each with only a single word or phrase written on it, but each representing countless memories and emotions that stretched all the way back to my childhood. I realised my hoarding hadn't started with the physical objects at all; my head was more crowded than my house, and if I wanted to let go of the stuff, then I had to let go of what was inside me first. I had to forgive myself. Nothing would go until I did.

I looked at my watch. I still had some time left before dinner, so I decided to use the watercolours to paint pictures over the words; if I was going to rid myself of all these horrible feelings then I might as well send them off in style. I tried to paint little scenes that represented the emotions behind the words but as I have no artistic skills whatsoever, by the time I'd finished all my pieces of paper looked like they'd been attacked by a four-year-old. I folded each one in four so that no one else could see my handiwork, laughing as I did so at the birds and love-hearts and terrible impressions of people that I'd tried to produce. Then I stacked the pile on my desk where it would sit until it was time for them all to be burnt.

I couldn't wait.

The next two days of yoga were much more enjoyable and, surprisingly, I could balance. I was a little freaked out to think that my mental instability had manifested itself physically. Adi laughed at me and said, 'Yes, Corinne. That's what yoga is all about.' Oh. Well at least I knew now. It occurred to me that the only person who hadn't lost their balance at all in the last four days was Vy.

On our final afternoon we made traditional offering baskets out of palm leaves. We then decorated them with flowers and set them aside. Adi lit a ceremonial fire in a woven basket in the middle of the yoga room and one at a time we threw in our pieces of paper. I had the most and the watercoloured pictures on them made them somewhat fire retardant. They took a long time to burn. I was too happy to feel self-conscious about it; I had not only spent a day really learning about myself, but I was now burning away all the parts I'd realised I shouldn't be holding on to. It felt great. I had not even made a copy of what I'd written on those bits of paper as a memento. I was finally, truly and completely letting go of something. Everyone waited patiently while my thoughts turned to embers and I added another few centimetres to the diameter of the hole in the ozone layer.

Vy had the fewest pieces of paper. She threw in two, and asked us if she'd done it right. When we said 'yes', she shrugged happily and started chatting about meeting her son-in-law at the airport when she got home.

We climbed back up the pebbled steps, through the frangipani and past half a dozen stone gods. We were on our way to the retreat's main altar to make our offerings. Vy was just in front of me, taking her time on the steep steps and stopping to inspect the plants as we passed. She fascinated me. Surely someone who was eighty years old had a million things in their life to let go of. Vy had only burnt two little pieces of paper. I tugged the sleeve of her kaftan.

'Hey, Vy, can I ask you something?'

She stopped and smiled at me. Now I felt shy.

'What did you do with your day of silence?'

'Oh, I slept. All of that walking—and the yoga is quite tiring.' She was still smiling at me.

'You didn't focus on getting rid of negative stuff, things you regret and so forth?'

'No!' She said it like I had just asked her if she was considering getting a boob job.

'Good grief, if I spent my time rattling around inside my own head thinking about things that I regretted, I would have missed all the lovely things going on around me. And then I really would've had something to regret.' She laughed and patted my hand like I was a simpleton. Which I guess I was.

Vy didn't come to the altar with us. Instead, she wandered back to her room, humming to herself.

When we got to the top of the steps we placed our little baskets of flower offerings in front of the Balinese god and stood back. Adi told us that if we wanted to, we could pray.

'Pray to this god, pray to your own god, pray to a butterfly called Brian if you like.' Adi giggled. 'What's important is that you pray sincerely. Whoever is supposed to hear it will do so if it comes from your heart.'

I prayed every night when I was a child. I prayed for my family, for my extended family, I prayed for all the children in my class at school, I prayed for the little girl in Waltons, I prayed for everyone I could remember and then I prayed for all the people I had probably forgotten. I used my prayers to cover all my bases, and as I grew older those prayers became longer and longer. Eventually, the burden of trying to remember everyone became too much and I stopped praying altogether. Ever since I was little, I've been rattling around inside my own head, focusing on the things I regret.

Now, standing at this altar, in front of a foreign god in a foreign country, I closed my eyes, clasped my hands to my forehead, thought of the god of my childhood, and for the first time in my life, I prayed for myself. I asked for help. I didn't feel guilty or selfish, I felt like it was about time. I opened my eyes and blinked. It felt like I had broken to the surface.

Chapter Fourteen

I had dinner on my own in Ubud that night, thinking over the last few days and congratulating myself on my decision to come to Bali. I felt light and free. I hadn't even succumbed to my usual sentimentality when I said goodbye to the others. Some of them, like Vy, I hadn't even seen before they left. I was okay with that. If I had learnt anything from Vy, I had learnt that the goodbye wasn't the important part, it was the time spent together that counted.

When I got back to the retreat, I passed the only other balcony I could see on the way up to my room. Dael was sitting out the front. I hadn't realised anyone else was staying on. As I made my way past, she waved me over.

She poured me a cup of ginger tea and I sat down awkwardly. Without Lucy or Vy or Adi to facilitate, I wasn't sure we had anything in common. Dael was stunning, with a short black bob, deep brown skin and the kind of body that made Halle Berry look like a frump. She was confident— almost outspoken—stylish and immaculately dressed. She spoke better English than I did. I was struggling to find common ground until she pulled out some gossip magazines. I instantly relaxed; bitching about celebrities had to be a universal language.

'Ugh.' I pulled a face. 'Britney Spears. What a bogan.'

Dael looked up from her magazine.

'What is a bogan?'

Okay. Maybe it wasn't as universal as I thought.

'It's an Australian term for someone who is uncultured. Sort of. It's not always a bad thing to be a bogan. Aussies celebrate their bogan tendencies.'

Dael looked at me blankly.

'Bogans wear T-shirts with pictures of Harley-Davidsons or Bon Jovi on the front.'

She was still looking at me blankly.

'They have mullets. You know, the hair that is short at the front and long at the back?'

'Oh!' She understood now. 'Like what the Americans call "white trash"?'

'Sort of.' I was drowning here. 'Sort of like white trash except bogans can be rich. They don't often live in trailers either. It's hard to explain. You'd have to see one to understand.'

'I move down to Legian tomorrow for a week. Maybe you could come there one day and show me.'

'Where's Legian?'

'It's near Kuta.'

'Oh. Okay. You're going to see a lot of bogans then.'

'Maybe I don't know what you are talking about because we don't have bogans at home.'

I doubted that. Every country has bogans, they just call them different things.

'I think you do, Dael—there must be people in the Netherlands that the rest of you laugh at and think look a bit daggy.'

'No.' Dael shook her head decisively. 'Every Dutch person has class. We don't have bogans. What is "daggy"?'

Suddenly Lucy burst through the foliage, suitcase and sunhat in hand.

Her fiancé had booked her on the wrong flight and she was stuck here for another two days. She admonished us for drinking tea instead of cocktails, sat down and regaled us with the story of her trip back into town.

'The taxi driver kept asking me if I wanted to go to a bar with him. Can you imagine it? I said I was getting married and he just shrugged and said he was married too and it didn't make any difference! Can you *imagine* that? So I panicked, and I'm sorry, Dael, but I told him that I was secretly a lesbian and I was coming back here to see you. That turned him off.'

I held up my hand.

'Let me get this clear, Lucy. You, with your long dark hair and perky little body told your driver that you were having a lesbian affair with Little Miss Hot Stuff over here, and the driver was turned *off*? Is Bali in topsy-turvy land?'

'Maybe it was against his religion.'

'And cheating wasn't? Which driver was this?'

Lucy told us and Dael instantly exclaimed that he had come on to her as well. In fact, it seemed that he had hit on nearly all of the women he had driven around. It was the same driver who had picked me up from the airport on my first night in town. Forty-five minutes I had spent in his car, and he didn't make a single move. Knowing my luck, he'd probably even had a crack at Vy.

Dael moved down to Legian the next day, and Lucy was going to bunk with her until her plane left. I was staying in the sleepier town of Ubud, intending to spend my time doing worthy things: visiting temples, art shops and cafés, perhaps I'd take a batik class. Dael and Lucy wrinkled their noses at my plans and insisted I come down and meet up with them the next night for dinner. I shyly accepted their offer.

The next night we went to the beachside fish restaurants in Jimbaran. We picked a restaurant at random and wandered out onto the sand. All the tables and chairs were set up directly on the beach and the sun was setting as we took our place near the water's edge. Tourists wandered past buying hot, coal-smoked corn from vendors with barbecues on wheeled carts. Two children were attempting to fly a kite in the dying dusk wind. We ordered lobsters and mussels and Long Island Iced Teas and settled back. Now I really felt like I was on holidays. Here I was, timid little me, sitting on a tropical beach with two complete strangers, sharing a meal and laughing and chatting like a normal person. I secretly wondered how long it would take for the jig to be up.

We left the restaurant late and went out the front where all the drivers were lined up, touting for business. We tried to find one who would make the hour-long trip back to Ubud but no one would do it for less than double the price I had paid to come in. I tried to negotiate, feebly, saying I could get a hotel room in Kuta for less money. They shrugged and walked away. Dael said, 'Well if it's cheaper to stay here, why don't you? Why not come back to Legian with us and we'll find you a hotel room?'

I didn't have a toothbrush or deodorant and the staff at the bed and breakfast I was staying at would be worried when I didn't turn up. I was meant to be taking a cooking class the next morning, then I wanted to do some washing and answer my emails and check my list of things-to-do to make sure I was on track and not going to miss out on anything. Then I stopped myself. I was rattling around inside my own head again, worried about things I might possibly regret. Hadn't I just decided to stop this kind of behaviour?

Just a few metres down the road from where Dael and Lucy were staying we found a rundown hotel that charged less than fifteen Australian dollars a night—with good reason. Looking around at the other clientele (middle-aged men with young, heavily made-up local girls on their arms) I guessed I was the only person who was hiring a room for the whole night. I took my key from the receptionist, found my room, shoved the door open with the help of a little light kicking, and walked inside. I checked everything out. Neither the shower nor the hot water tap in the bathroom sink worked. I laughed. I supposed that this was what letting go was all about.

The next day, I half-showered under the cold tap and called the owner of the B&B to reassure him that I was alive. Then I put on the knickers that I had washed the night before and hung over the bedside lamp to dry and strolled up the road to have breakfast with Dael and Lucy. The two of them were going to spend the day shopping and they asked me to join them. I hesitated. I was a hoarder, I didn't need the temptation.

'Come on!' Dael laughed. 'You have to show me a bogan!'

We spent the day wandering in and out of boutiques. I bought two sarongs, a toothbrush and a pair of sandals to replace the heels I was hobbling around in from the night before. Then I bought some Bandaids to cover the blisters that the new sandals caused. I did not buy any trashy souvenirs or postcards to remind me of the area, nor did I take photographs of every shop we passed for a scrapbook I would never make. Instead, I enjoyed the moment and hung out with my new friends.

I had bought everything extremely cheaply and that was no doubt due to the fact that I hadn't done any of the bargaining myself. Lucy had been to Bali numerous times and assured us she knew the right price for everything. I was happy to stand back and let her do the negotiating; it meant I didn't have to do any thinking, something which I was starting to enjoy. Lucy was ferocious, putting on a show that made Sharon Osbourne look like Bambi. She would roll her eyes, clutch at her heart and yell, 'What are you *doing* to me? Do I look like a Japanese tourist? Do I look like I'm that easy? Local price! Local price!' Twice when Lucy wasn't looking, I snuck back into the shop we had just left and slipped the shop assistant an extra couple of dollars.

By midday it was too hot to shop any longer so we lunched at a beachside

Italian restaurant and fortified ourselves with cocktails. Dael looked out over the balcony, pointing at people and calling out loudly, 'Corinne, is that a bogan?'

Dael, I had discovered over the last day and a half, was one of those people who saw her opinions as facts. The night before she had grabbed my iPod, flicked through the song list and pronounced, 'You are listening to the wrong music,' before pulling out the headphones and putting it back in my handbag.

At breakfast that morning I had tried the traditional rice *bubur* that was a staple of the Balinese diet. Dael stared open-mouthed at the porridge-like substance in front of me.

'You cannot eat that for breakfast!'

'The Balinese do, Dael. I'm sure if it's good enough for them, it's good enough for me.'

'Well, that is just crazy and they are wrong.' I couldn't help laughing at her horrified expression.

Now, she was leaning over the balcony and pointing at a pale young man in a sleeveless T-shirt. 'That one with the bad hair! Is that a bogan?'

He looked up and I pulled Dael back into her seat. 'Shhhh!' I whispered. 'No, he's just English.'

After lunch we had a massage, all together in the one room. As I undressed, Dael frowned, pointed at my underpants and said, 'This is why you are single.' For once, her point was fair. Hoarding ancient underwear was one thing, wearing it was quite another.

That night we had more cocktails at the hotel bar overlooking Kuta beach. Lucy was to leave in a few hours' time and I was finally going to head back to Ubud. We talked about how much we were going to miss each other and what a great time we'd had. Dael laughed. It was her first time overseas on her own and she couldn't believe that she had managed to land on her feet so well. Lucy smiled and said, 'You two should buddy up for the rest of your time here.'

Dael and I looked at each other.

'Why not?' Lucy encouraged. 'You're both on your own, you have no plans, there's no reason to go your separate ways.'

Dael looked expectant. I wanted to say no. I did have plans. In fact, I had an exhaustive list of things I wanted to do in Bali—there was a temple I wanted to see, a cookery class I wanted to take, a traditional dance show I wanted to attend. I had drawn up a timetable with carefully allotted hours for each activity and I was going to have trouble fitting in everything as it was. If I buddied up with Dael I would have to compromise and I did not want to miss something and regret it later. I was just about to say that I couldn't join her and then I stopped myself. There was a real human being sitting opposite me, a real-life, possibly crazy, human being. Surely the experiences we would have together would be more fun than ticking stuff off a stupid list.

'Sure thing. Dael, you up for it?'

'Of course! But you can't wear that dress again, Corinne. It is bad.'

As the sun set, we watched the parade of tourists stroll past on the road that divided us from the beach. There were families, young couples, old couples, newlyweds. Then I saw a couple with matching mullets. They were so tanned they looked like they were getting ready to enter a George Hamilton look-alike contest. Their hair was almost white from what was probably a combination of too much sun and household bleach. The woman was wearing a bikini one size too small and it was struggling to stretch across her enormous bosom. The man was wearing nothing but a pair of fluorescent pink Speedos, his enormous leathery brown gut hanging down over the front, but not far enough to hide the most enormous pair of testicles I had ever seen. They knocked back and forth inside his Speedos like an executive desk toy. It was almost hypnotic. I snapped out of it and punched Dael in the arm.

'Dael!' I pointed in their direction. 'Bogans!'

As she looked up, they started talking loudly to each other in what sounded like Italian.

'No!' Dael said. 'No!'

'What?' Lucy and I said it at the same time.

'They are Dutch!'

It was the only time I ever saw Dael distressed the whole time we spent together.

Lucy left on a late flight and I grabbed a car back to Ubud. Before going our separate ways the three of us hugged and promised to meet up again. The next morning I packed up my hotel room, checked out, threw my list in the bin and moved down to share Dael's room in Legian. I felt so carefree that I rang the airline and extended my trip by another two days.

Dael and I sunbathed, took a surfing class and went white-water rafting. The only nod to my now-abandoned list was an afternoon spent visiting an art museum. I did this on my own while Dael let herself get spectacularly ripped off by a guy selling fake watches on the street.

'But he came to the cash machine with me and showed me how much money to withdraw!' Dael was protesting against my scepticism. 'He was very helpful!'

'I have absolutely no doubt about that Dael, but the watch isn't even working.'

She rolled her eyes and looked at me with sympathy. 'Well of course not,' she said. 'they are special watches that work off the energy in your body. I have to wear it for a while for the electricity to build up inside.' And then she carefully packed it away.

That night, we were going out nightclubbing. I desperately did not want to go, but as I had convinced Dael to go white-water rafting with me the day before, I now owed her a favour in return. I have never liked nightclubs. There's too much noise, the people are too drunk, the prices for drinks are ridiculous and they never, ever play any Bruce Springsteen. I used to go when I was a teenager but only because if I had said that I preferred to go somewhere quiet where we could have a nice conversation, my friends would have shrunk away from me like I had tuberculosis. The only way I'd got through it was to drink so much I thought I was somewhere else.

I chose the quietest, most deserted nightclub I could find. Dael wrinkled her nose at me and I tried to avoid making eye contact with her.

'It'll fill up soon, it's just because we're here so early.' I hoped I was lying.

Dael moved onto the dance floor and started jiggling to the music. She was the only one out there. I watched our handbags. I wasn't cool and carefree anymore, I was back in high school, sitting on the sidelines trying to pretend I liked it. The jig was finally up. I lost sight of Dael and when she reappeared, she had two men in tow. They were carrying drinks for us.

'They are French! This one is called . . . actually I don't know. It's too loud in here. I think that one—' she pointed at the taller of the two '—is called Van Damme.'

Van Damme grinned shyly.

I smiled politely at the Frenchmen, waited for Dael to sip her drink and when she didn't fall unconscious, I sipped mine as well.

It turned out neither of them spoke perfect English and unless we were booking a single train ticket to Calais or needed to find the nearest *école*, my French was going to be useless. But they seemed sweet, so Van Damme and I spent a delightful twenty minutes yelling into each other's ears and saying 'Pardon?' a lot which, thankfully, meant the same thing in both languages.

Dael didn't let the language barrier stop her at all and gabbled away happily to Van Damme's friend, who had the more plausible name of Fab. He didn't say anything in response, he just stood there grinning. Dael was wearing a pair of tight, low-cut white jeans and an equally tight, low-cut white top. If I was a man, I wouldn't have cared what she was saying either.

'We went white-water rafting yesterday and Corinne head-butted a Korean!'

That was not strictly true. I didn't head-butt him, I fell backwards in the raft and smashed my helmeted head into his face. He was very polite about it and there was no blood.

'Then we went surfing and she cried!' Dael was laughing.

Okay. That was definitely not true. I got dumped by a wave, hit in the head with the surfboard and I inhaled a lot of salt water. I wasn't crying, I was choking. Mostly. Thankfully, because it was so loud, neither of the Frenchmen was able to understand what Dael was saying.

Van Damme and I moved to the back of the nightclub and found somewhere quiet where we could almost hear each other. It didn't really help as neither of us had spontaneously learnt the other person's language in the few metres we had covered. In the end, we amused ourselves by teaching each other the names of various diseases in our own languages. By pointing at imaginary dots all over my face and pretending to scratch at them, I found out that chicken pox is called *varicelle*, and by miming first my hands and then my legs falling off, I discovered leprosy is called *lèpre*. Van Damme told me the French word for herpes is *herpes*, you just had to say it like you were Pepe Le Pew. Thankfully he knew that off the top of his head and he didn't attempt to act it out. Although yelling 'Erpeez!' in a crowded nightclub was probably not endearing him to anyone except me. Eventually, we ran out of illnesses we could successfully mime. I tried for measles, but it looked too much like chicken pox and Van Damme was getting frustrated because I couldn't figure out what illness involved flapping like a bird. We were struggling for something else to talk about when his face lit up and he said, 'Ahh! The French word for the seal—you know,' he clapped the backs of his hands together and made a honking sound, 'the animal of the sea, yes? The French word for that is *phoque*.' It sounded exactly like 'fuck' and I laughed like a child. Apparently Van Damme and I shared the same infantile sense of humour.

At the end of the night Dael and I exchanged phone numbers with our new French friends and promised to have dinner with them the next night. I would never do something like this in Australia. In fact, I would never do something like this anywhere. Normally I would have come up with a million reasons not to have dinner with two complete strangers with whom I had to mime to be understood. This was a mixture of Dael's influence and a clear-cut case of the holiday crazies. Still, it was a lot more fun than sitting in my hotel room, consulting a list and deciding whether I would spend the next day visiting an agricultural museum or attending a lecture on the principles of Balinese shadow puppetry. And besides, Van Damme had the bluest eyes I had ever seen.

Lying in bed mulling over everything that had happened since I'd arrived, I realised I had not mentioned Thomas, the Bastard Man or my miserable house full of stuff to anyone else, not even once. It hadn't occurred to me to do so. I was enjoying being the kind of person who didn't have baggage, the kind of person who just got on with life and enjoyed the moment. The best part was, I wasn't pretending to be someone else. Freed from all of that, I really was a person who enjoyed life and making new friends and doing stupid things. Maybe when I got home I would be brave enough to throw out some of my crap. Maybe I could be this person all the time.

Dael and I turned up to the restaurant early the next evening and toasted each other with champagne. This was going to be our last night together. Dael went back home tomorrow and I moved to Nusa Dua for one final night. Van Damme and Fab turned up and we did that European kissing-on-each-cheek thing that I always messed up by saying 'Mwaaah!' loudly into the ears of the person I was kissing. After I had finished deafening everyone we went to our table. The good thing about travelling with someone as effervescent as Dael is that you are never stuck for conversation. Without the Mojitos and the noise of the nightclub, Van Damme, Fab and I were all too shy to know what to say. If it had not been for Dael, we probably would have eaten in silence and then left.

'So Van Damme . . . Van Damme?' He was not paying any attention. Dael tapped him on the arm. 'Van Damme?'

'Me? My name is Jordan.' Jordan laughed. 'You think I am called Van Damme? Like the action man?' He laughed again and pretended to karate chop a bread roll. He explained everything in rapid French to Fab and then we were all laughing and Dael was flicking her wrist and saying, 'Who cares?'

We ate and drank and Dael waved her fork around and chastised Jordan and Fab for not listening to the right music, not going to the right clubs and for living in the wrong part of France. Eventually she and Fab wandered out of the restaurant and down to the beach for a cigarette. Left on our own, Jordan and I were struggling, yet again, to find something to talk about. After a few minutes' silence he asked what kind of music I listened to. I tried to think of a band or composer that he would know. Satie? No, I would sound like a wanker. Bruce Springsteen? No, I wouldn't be able to cope if he disapproved. Belle and Sebastian? No, they just sounded French because of their names. Then I remembered the one French singer I knew apart from Maurice Chevalier.

'Do you know Camille? I love her.'

It wasn't a lie. After hearing one of her songs on the radio I had immediately bought the album, even though she sang in French and I couldn't understand a word of it. I listened to it over and over again and finally, when the curiosity became too great, I attempted to translate the lyrics. I used my old French textbooks and dictionaries from school (priding myself on the fact that I had not thrown them away) and I watched *Amelie* again just in case one of the characters happened to say something similar to the lyrics in any of the songs. When I was still left with gaping holes, I jumped online and found a translation website. I suspected that it was not really giving me the right answers when it translated 'La jeune fille aux cheveux blancs'—a song title I was pretty sure meant 'the young girl with white hair'—as 'the rats are eating mess tarts'.

Jordan's eyes lit up when I mentioned her name.

'She is my favourite!'

That was the kind of luck I never hit upon. Jordan and I spent the rest of the night talking about Camille and writing down the names of bands that we thought the other one would like. We swapped email addresses and he suggested meeting up again the next night. I looked at him. He was beautiful. How far exactly was I willing to take this whole holiday crazies thing? Almost as quickly as the idea came to me, I dismissed it. He was not only cute, he was also a really genuine and sweet man. It seemed impolite to use him as a human dildo. Part of letting go is knowing when enough is enough.

Before I went to bed that night Jordan sent me a text. 'I had fun *ma jolie australienne*.' I was happy to let go of a lot of things in Bali but I was keeping that message.

The next morning Dael and I held each other for a long time and both of us had tears in our eyes when we said goodbye.

'Please keep in touch.' Dael wiped at her eyes. 'And please get better underpants.'

When she left, I felt at a loss. I pulled out my phone and looked at the message from Jordan again. I nearly called him. Nearly. And then I packed my bags and moved down to Nusa Dua to spend one final day completely by myself, eating, sleeping and working on my tan. I would be fine on my own.

My favourite Camille song is called 'Pour que l'Amour me Quitte'. I had translated this myself as 'Until the Love Leaves Me', which Jordan had told me was more or less correct. I was so excited to find someone else who loved Camille's music (and more importantly, knew what she was singing) that I had grilled him relentlessly on all the words and phrases in all the songs that I had not been able to decipher. I doubt translators at the United Nations worked as hard as he did that night. There were only two words in 'Pour que l'Amour me Quitte' that I had not been able to figure out: *pagayer* and *décrocher*.

'Well, the first means this,' and Jordan had mimed paddling. 'So, in the song, she is doing this away from her broken heart. Yes? And the second, *décrocher*, this is harder for me.' He frowned and his blue eyes swept across the restaurant and out to the beach.

'It has many meanings, but in this song, it means "letting go".'

Even the French were telling me it was time.

Chapter Fifteen

The cold blast of Melbourne's mid-autumnal air whistled past my ears as I stood outside Tullamarine airport, suitcase in hand, looking for a taxi. I thought that arriving back home would be miserable—the end of a holiday usually is—but not this time. This time I wanted to jump out of the cab at every shop I knew and run inside calling out, 'I'm home! And guess what? I've got my shit together!'

I'd been a pile of self-absorption for too long. Now that I'd burnt away all the bad bits, I was ready to start anew. Even walking into my overstuffed apartment couldn't depress me; I knew what kind of person I could be if everything went and I liked that girl. I wanted to give her room to breathe.

I didn't waste any time. As soon as I'd unpacked and called Adam to tell him I was home, I opened my wardrobe and pulled out the first box I laid my hands on. This time, I asked myself questions as I went, calling to mind how good I felt in Bali. Did my stash of novelty socks make me feel adventurous and spontaneous? No. Out they went. Did the fluorescent pink blush I wore in the mid-eighties say anything about the person that I wanted to become? Definitely not. Out. What did the street directory from my first car say about me? It said I was a hoarder. Burn it. I was an archaeologist excavating my own life, determined to dig myself out of the rubble. Within a week I had cleared out half of my wardrobe and it was neither painful nor arduous. It was liberating.

I stood back and surveyed my handiwork. Even though I had achieved so much, I was a little disappointed by what I saw; a lot of stuff had still gone back into boxes. I had a feeling that I probably wasn't being as brutal as I could be. Still, I'd thrown away more than I ever had in the past. It was a monumental start.

As I was going through a pile of photographs, the phone rang.

'Hey, it's Jonathan.'

Did I know a Jonathan?

'From Canberra. We met at that pub?'

'Oh! Yes. Right.'

What? I vaguely remembered meeting him at some party or other. He worked for the government or the United Nations or *Today Tonight*, I couldn't remember which. Obviously I'd thought enough of our conversation to give him my number because here he was now, cheerfully babbling away on the other end of the phone.

'I checked with the UN, and if you still want to go to Jordan and tour the refugee camps, I can arrange it for you.'

My eyebrows shot up so high, they hit the back of my neck. Clearly he thought he had rung Angelina Jolie. Had I really said I wanted to go to the Middle East and visit refugees? I cast my mind back about four months. Oh dear. Now I remembered. We had talked about asylum seekers in Australia and I had mentioned that it would be interesting to see what the conditions were like for these people in other countries. Jonathan had said that if I wanted, he could probably arrange for me to take a tour. I'd smiled enthusiastically and said that would be great. I never thought he would follow through, I was just being polite.

I looked around my flat uselessly, like I was expecting someone to leap out from behind the couch, take the phone from my hand and do the dirty work of letting this guy down on my behalf. When no one magically appeared, I scrunched up my face and murmured, 'Oh. Really? That's . . . great.'

How was I going to get out of this? I didn't want to go traipsing around dangerous, desert-riddled parts of the world. If I said that out loud, however, he might think I was heartless. On the other hand, maybe he didn't care what I said. He'd probably only made one phone call.

'Yeah, I put a lot of work into it and rang a lot of people. They need to know quickly though. So, you still want to go?'

I broke out in a sweat.

'Sure, of course!'

About seven years ago I had parachuted out of a helicopter because a friend had called me a coward when I'd said I didn't want to. Now I was agreeing to go to a Middle Eastern country that bordered Iraq—on my own—because I didn't want someone I had met once to think I was insincere. Obviously I had a lot more problems than just hoarding.

I hung up the phone and calmed myself down. This should be easy to sort out; I had a couple of weeks up my sleeve, that was enough time in which to come up with a plausible excuse. Perhaps I could say that I couldn't afford to go—although I didn't want him to think that I was poor. Or I could say that I was busy—although I didn't want him to think that I believed myself more important than refugees. Or perhaps I could say that my mother was sick—although I was too superstitious to say that in case it came true.

When he rang back a week later I still didn't have a good lie prepared, so I half-heartedly mumbled my way through a conversation about dates of arrival and departure. Then I started getting emails from a woman at the Office of the United Nations High Commissioner for Refugees, asking me to explain the purpose of my trip, what I wanted to achieve, who I wanted to see. She was very businesslike and very intelligent and about to be seconded to the most-recently bombed part of Pakistan. Now I had to say yes so that I didn't appear flaky. The trouble was, I *was* flaky; I had a drawer full of bookmarks from Sunday School that I didn't dare throw out in case Jesus saw me do it.

In the end I agreed to go to Jordan because I was too gutless to say no. Perhaps it would be good for me. After all, I had come home from Bali promising myself to embrace adventure and on top of that, the spooky coincidence of meeting a man called Jordan in Bali and now being presented with the opportunity to travel to a country of the same name felt like kismet.

Feeling as if I was falling from a great height, I cancelled the show I was supposed to be doing in Perth and booked the flights. I got myself a visa for Jordan, I booked into a tiny hotel somewhere in the suburbs of Amman—the kind of thing a suicide bomber wouldn't consider a worthwhile target—and updated my will. I also applied for life insurance and travel insurance and wrote my blood type on the top left-hand corner of my passport, the inside of my wallet and my driver's licence. I had to work hard to stop myself from writing it on the waistband of all my underpants as well.

Four weeks later, I was standing in line in Queen Alia International Airport some time after midnight (sober this time), wearily holding out my passport and visa and hoping I was in the right country. Thanks to the vagaries of using air miles to book a round-the-world ticket, my trip had taken forty hours. I was beyond discombobulated. At around the thirty-hour mark I had started to hallucinate. I am positive that I watched a kitten eat a tarantula on the in-flight entertainment system. I can remember thinking that it seemed odd that a kitten would be out in the desert like that, on its own, eating giant spiders. It was unnerving. It was like watching a six-year-old girl in a party dress gnaw on a raw leg of lamb.

As with Bali, arriving at night meant that I couldn't get my bearings.

As the taxi driver headed for Amman, I squinted out the window. Apart from the highway we were driving along, it was almost completely dark. At least the road signs were in Arabic, reassuring me that I was in the right country. Or near it.

My hopefully terrorist-proof hideaway was sequestered in a middle-class residential area and we arrived at it via a bamboozling array of one-way streets, winding up and down hills past large houses, apartment blocks and what appeared to be a wooded park, locked behind a high barbed-wire fence. When we arrived I saw an unadorned, cream-coloured three-storey building. I unloaded my bags, climbed the two steps to the entrance and proceeded through the metal detector in the doorway. There was no separate place for my luggage to pass, so I dragged it through the detector as well. I set off the alarm. I stood just inside the lobby, waiting for someone to come over and search me. Instead, the tired-looking night clerk impatiently beckoned me towards him. I looked doubtfully at the metal detector, moved inside and checked in.

Another man wearing a *shmagh mhadab*—the red and white headscarf—took me up to my room and pointed out every item in there, naming them as he went. He named the stove, the shower, the toilet, the pillows, the light fittings—maybe he was practising his English. I was barely able to stand straight from exhaustion and when he had finished, I smiled politely, showed him the door and lay down on the bed, thankful for the sparseness of the room. If he had been showing me around my own place, we would have been up all night.

At dawn I was woken by the sounds of the nearest muezzin calling out the *adhān*—the Muslim call to prayer. The air was so still and so quiet that the singing sounded like it was right outside my window. Even though I had only been asleep for two hours, I slid out of bed, padded over to the window and pulled back the curtain. I have no idea what I expected to see, since it was just before dawn and still dark. There were no cars on the streets, no

people walking around. Apart from the streetlamps reflecting off the coni-
fers in front of me I couldn't see any other lights. People must have been
awake in most of the buildings, including the hotel rooms on either side of
me, and yet there was no indication of them. I sat there and listened to the
prayer and I could almost see it gently dropping over the whole city. Each
phrase spread out and dissipated and dissolved back into silence before the
next line started. It was easy to see the beauty in a faith that started each day
with such reverence. I went back to bed and stared at the ceiling; I had never
been anywhere this foreign. I was too excited to sleep.

That morning I helped myself to the breakfast buffet of hard-boiled
eggs, hummus and flatbread. As I ate, I scoured my guidebook for something to do. I had not made lists in advance, but with only two days until
I met up with my UN contact, I wanted to make the most of my free
time. Today, I had decided to take a taxi to the National Archaeological
Museum. It sat upon the highest point in Amman and held a collection of
the Dead Sea Scrolls. The opportunity to see them felt unbelievable, like
someone had told me I could go the North Pole and visit Santa. I'd always
been fascinated by the Dead Sea Scrolls. It wasn't just their antiquity; it
was the influence they'd had on the world that tickled my imagination.
And also, if I was honest with myself, a small part of me wanted to believe
that if they were worth holding on to, then perhaps everything else was
as well. Maybe, just maybe, I wasn't a hoarder after all; maybe I was the
custodian of future priceless artefacts.

The guidebook I had brought with me had a long chapter on Middle
Eastern etiquette and I read it worriedly as I chewed on the last of my flatbread. There was a lot to remember, including that I should only ever use
my right hand to pass and receive things. This was going to be a problem.
I am left-handed. Having to use my right side for anything was going
to leave me looking like a stroke victim. There were also an inordinate
number of things that women couldn't do. I knew that I should dress

modestly and not cuss like a sailor but I hadn't realised that I would not be allowed to enter many of the cafés and restaurants in town because I was unaccompanied by a man. I huffed with exasperation, then immediately chastised myself. I was in another country and I had chosen to come here of my own accord; I should let go of my prejudices and try to embrace this new culture without judgement. Or, at the very least, I should save my whingeing for when I got back home.

A tall moustachioed man at reception rang me a taxi and I passed through the metal detector—setting it off once again—and out onto the street to await its arrival. I could have sat inside but all the lounges were occupied by men and my guidebook said that custom forbade me from sharing a seat with anyone of the opposite sex. If I had wanted to sit down I would have had to stare expectantly at one of the males until he stood up. Considering that I was only in this country because I hadn't been game to say 'no' on the telephone, the chance of me squaring my shoulders and staring down a bunch of local men was about as likely as Steven Seagal winning an Academy Award.

When my driver turned up he gave me a broad smile. I instinctively wanted to shake his hand in greeting but at the last moment—thanks once again to my guidebook—I held back. I was in a country where consensual sex between an unmarried couple could lead to three years in prison. If I was going to go around trying to shake hands with men, I may as well dress up like Dolly Parton in *Best Little Whorehouse in Texas* and randomly ask strangers to slap my behind.

We wound back down the confusing array of residential streets, past white apartment block after white apartment block, and out onto the major freeways. Amman was what I had expected a Middle Eastern city to look like: almost monochromatic and lacking vegetation. Still, the lack of any grass whatsoever— even on empty blocks of land—was a shock to my dainty little Western eyes.

The taxi could not take me up to the museum entrance, so instead my driver dropped me at the entrance gate a few hundred metres away from it. I got out and started the hot trek uphill. I wished I had remembered to bring a bottle of water with me. Even early in the morning, the sun was scorching and the air was dry. The scarf I had loosely wrapped over my head to conceal my hair was already starting to irritate me and I could feel perspiration beading on the back of my neck. I was also wearing long pants and a long-sleeved shirt in an effort to appear modest. I hoped the museum would be air-conditioned.

I had expected that the view at the top of the hill would give me an idea of how Amman was laid out. It didn't. Stretching away as far as I could see were these unadorned, white cement buildings, piled on top of each other, climbing the sides of the barren hills and jumbled in what used to be valleys below. Occasionally, where the land was too steep to build, there was a patch of gritty beige-coloured earth. It looked like a construction site more than a city. There was no colour anywhere apart from the very occasional conifer. It went on and on like this, up and down the mountains to the horizon. There were a couple of straggly trees at the top of the hill I was standing on and I spent twenty minutes fiddling around with my camera, trying to frame up something vaguely picturesque.

I entered the museum. It was small, about the size of a two-bedroom Australian house. The display cases looked like the ones normally found in shops or libraries, not museums. There didn't seem to be an alarm system and some of the artefacts were simply resting on plinths, with not even a rope around them to stop people getting too close. A cat slunk past me and curled itself around the leg of a table. I stepped back, wondering if it was the kind that ate tarantulas.

I walked up to the first exhibit—a collection of sculptures—and read the perfunctory little piece of cardboard that described them. It turned out I was looking at some of the world's oldest sculptures. Six and a half thousand years ago, someone had made these doll-like, square-bodied, two-headed men and women. Somehow they had survived through the millennia and now they were here, in front of me. I couldn't fathom it.

I wandered past jewellery, bowls, carvings, all of them from a time that seemed implausible. Even though I was in the wrong country, I half expected to see accompanying photos of Elizabeth Taylor and Richard Burton on the set of *Cleopatra* using these objects as props. It was all so old and so delicate and so precious; *this* was the kind of stuff worth hanging on to. I wondered doubtfully if my stuff would become that valuable if it survived a few thousand years. I looked again at the collection in front of me. Nothing in it seemed to be the ancient equivalent of half a dozen novelty erasers and a legless Smurf figurine.

I ventured into a little room at the back of the museum, and there, right in front of me, were the Dead Sea Scrolls. It was like being in the presence of royalty. Perhaps it was because I was the only person in there, but the room felt like it had a presence of some sort. In fact, apart from one other man and his guide, I had the whole museum to myself. I could act as giddy and stupid as I liked. I took lots of photos; there were no signs to say that I couldn't. Along the right-hand side of the room were broken bits of what looked like a stone tablet. I stepped closer to read the explanation. Surprisingly, they were the stone benches on which the scrolls were written. How did they know that? There was nothing to explain further, the sign said simply 'Tables and benches on which the scrolls were written'. There were no ropes in front of them, no warnings not to touch. I looked around and then reached out and put my hand on the place where another person had sat over two thousand years before to etch out some of the most controversial and famous documents in existence. I stood very still, appreciating the moment. It put my belongings into perspective. Even if everything I owned survived two thousand years, I didn't own one thing that would come close to the objects in this room.

I passed back through the museum, taking a final look at everything before I left. All of these documents, artefacts, sculptures and jewels were laid out so modestly. There were no gaudy signs and flashing lights, no audio guides or velveteen ropes to let people know they were looking at Something Important. I was reminded of the city view I had seen outside—I was in a part of the world where people didn't tart things up. Instead, they simply laid out everything and let it tell its own story. My collection of Teenage Mutant Ninja Turtle memorabilia, carefully arranged along the tops of my bookshelves and linked together with an old bit of tinsel, started to seem a little tacky.

I lay in bed that night staring at the ceiling. Thanks to jet lag I couldn't sleep. It seemed that I had just drifted off when the dawn *adhān* woke me again. I flicked on the bedside lamp, pulled out my trusty guidebook and skimmed through the places I was going to visit that day. I had splurged the night before and booked a car and driver. In a few hours' time I was going to travel down to the Dead Sea for a swim and then I was going to take in some other sights near the King's Highway, a road so ancient it was mentioned in the Bible. Like the day before, it all seemed too extraordinary to be real.

My driver, Hana, arrived promptly at 10 a.m. in his shiny black car with cream leather seats. I climbed in the back, luxuriating in the air-conditioning. He didn't smile when I greeted him like my last driver had, he just shut the car door on me, climbed in the front and started driving. I sat in the back, feeling like I was in trouble for something. I flicked through my guidebook. Had I used my left hand? Had I greeted him inappropriately? Had I sat in such a way that I was showing him the sole of my shoe? I couldn't figure out what I'd done wrong. I decided to stay still and keep my mouth shut.

Cruising through an upmarket residential area, I spied a middle-aged man herding some goats. There were no fields, sheds or farms anywhere near us, just houses and roads. My resolve to keep quiet disappeared; this was too strange not to query. I summoned up my courage and called out to Hana: 'Excuse me, why does that man have goats?'

Did he sell them door-to-door perhaps?

'The goats are for the beautiful.'

'Pardon?'

Hana said it again like I was an idiot.

'The beautiful! The *goats* are for the *beautiful.*'

I wasn't game to ask again, and considering my Arabic consisted of nothing more than the word for 'thank you', I didn't expect I would be able to get a better answer. '*Shukran,*' I said meekly. Hana did not seem like the kind of guy who would enjoy miming out the word for measles. I preferred my theory anyway; that the goatherd was selling his animals door-to-door, like a meaty version of the Avon lady.

As we drew closer to the Dead Sea we passed a few luxury hotels built on what used to be the edge of the water but which were now a few metres back from it. Hana told me that, thanks to heavy irrigation along its tributaries, the sea was shrinking and in forty years it was expected to disappear altogether. These posh hotels, with their palm-tree gardens and expensive European cars lined up out the front, were resting on the edges of murky, eroded banks with nothing around them at all. It looked a little like a movie version of the aftermath of a nuclear war.

After about an hour's drive, Hana pulled into a car park and brusquely led me through a shaded archway where I paid for our tickets. Then we passed into the bright sunshine of the resort. There was a large swimming pool, surrounded by flat stone pavers and one solitary palm tree. To both my left and right were rocky hills, covered in dirt and not much else. The pool was built up a couple of metres from the beach and on the other side of it the stone paving dropped away abruptly. I could see the Dead Sea and, beyond, a barren mountain range. Even though I was standing at the lowest point on earth, I felt like I was about to go swimming on the moon.

I found the change rooms—full of pale European women—and changed into my swimmers. I didn't bother with sunscreen; the heaviness of the atmosphere, combined with the haze evaporating off the surface of the water, was supposed to provide a natural UV barrier. I pulled at my two-piece swimming costume, trying to get it to cover the little bit of belly that was sticking out between the top and bottom halves. After the last couple of days of wearing long-sleeved shirts, long pants and a scarf over my head, it felt weird to be so exposed. Outside I passed a gift shop that sold Muslim swimming costumes, all-in-one suits that reached from neck to ankle with a little frill around the waist. I rearranged my sarong to cover as much of me as I could and pitter-pattered past the swimming pool and concession stand to the steps leading down to the water's edge.

The beach was very rocky and the sea was the same steel-grey colour as the sky. A replica Bedouin tent was set up on the far side of the complex, and on the other side was some wire, separating us from the desert. On the boundary closest to me stood a donkey tethered under a lean-to. It had its back to everyone and was staring resolutely at the stone wall in front of it, as if it wanted nothing to do with the tomfoolery going on behind it.

I gingerly picked my way across the beach and walked into the sea. All around me people were squealing and laughing as they lifted their feet from the sea floor and flipped unexpectedly onto their backs. There was so much salt in the water that it was impossible to sink. One young Muslim girl walked into the water fully clothed. She didn't even take off her belt. I wondered how much fun she was having trying to swim in denim jeans. I walked in until I was chest-high in the water. I didn't feel light, as I had expected, so I lifted my feet from the ground. Instantly, I flipped onto my back like everyone else, with my knees sticking out of the water in front of me. I gasped. Without having to try to stay afloat at all, I flipped myself over onto my stomach and half swam, half dragged myself out a little further so I could stand upright in the water with my feet not touching the ground. I hung there, bobbing like a cork. Whenever I caught someone else's eye, we grinned at each other like idiots. I was an astronaut of the sea. I bobbed around for a while, being careful not to get the water in my eyes as I had read that it stung like crazy. I couldn't resist licking my lips though. I wanted to know how intense thirty per cent salt water tasted. I stuck out my tongue and pulled a face. It didn't taste like salt, it tasted bitter and chemically.

I floated back to shore. There were buckets of black mud dotted along the beach and people were digging in and covering themselves in the stuff. It was supposed to be very good for the skin. I went up to a bucket and started slopping it on. And then I got yelled at.

'Three dinar! Three dinar!'

I scampered off to get my handbag, followed all the way by the angry yelling man. I kept my head down and ignored him until I found my wallet and carefully pulled out the notes. I went back and continued covering myself in the mud as if nothing had happened. Then an old bloke came up to me, stuck his hand in the bucket and egged on by his male friends, slapped it on my back. They all giggled and I frowned at him. This was not appropriate behaviour at all. Before I had left Australia, a friend who spoke Arabic had taught me the word *haraam*, which roughly translates as 'a thing that the Koran does not allow'. Apparently you would instantly shame the person you said it to but even now, as this old fellow accosted me, I wasn't prepared to go that far. I let myself be groped first on the back and then, bizarrely, in my armpit because I didn't want to appear like a rude Westerner. Instead I waggled my finger at him and told him that was enough.

I sat in the sun until the mud dried on my body, pondering the fact that I had chosen political correctness over stopping someone from molesting me. Then I thought about it: was it political correctness, or was I chicken? I had thought that I was just scared to throw my stuff out but maybe I was scared of everything: scared of offending people, scared of appearing rude or stupid, or insulting. That old bloke wasn't the idiot, I was. It was about time I grew a backbone.

I went back into the water and washed off the mud. Hana was waiting for me and, when I was dried and dressed, he loudly insisted I visit the souvenir shop. I guessed that he probably got a commission if I bought anything. I walked in the door and stood there without looking at a thing and instead, stared at him. 'Bugger it,' I thought. 'If he's going to act like a bully, I'll act like a bully back.' Eventually he got the idea and we walked back out. Even though my behaviour was completely passive-aggressive, it was a start. I gave myself an imaginary pat on the back.

We drove up the mountain to a geological museum called the Dead Sea Panorama. Hana told me I had one hour. I told him I might be longer and walked off before he could argue. I giggled to myself when I knew he wasn't looking. I felt like a naughty schoolgirl.

Inside was an elaborate exhibition. There were glass display cases, electronic displays with little lights on them, a diorama of the area and a video display. I perused everything slowly, reading about the history of the land and how the Dead Sea had formed in a fault in the earth's crust millions of years before. Beneath the Dead Sea, two massive tectonic plates met and, much like the inhabitants living on top of them, they were grating against each other. On the Jordanian side the plate was moving north, on the Israeli side it was going south. Never let it be said that the Middle Eastern conflict is only on the surface; it goes right down to the centre of the earth.

I peered at displays of insects and wildlife, taxidermied animals and bits of rock. I found a table showing the chemical composition of the Dead Sea; it turned out it wasn't just full of salt, it also contained 7800 times more cadmium than normal sea water and 94 times more bromine. When

I had licked my lips I had probably licked my way to a tumour.

I left the museum after an hour and a quarter and headed towards the car. I had a bottle of water in there and I suddenly had an urge to drink all of it. As I opened the passenger-side door and went to get in, Hana shook his head and pointed down in front of the complex.

'You should see this,' and he grinned for the first time that day. Obviously my timid first steps at standing up for myself had not caused the world to cave in.

We walked the short distance down a pathway and when we stopped, I instinctively shied back. To my left, the rocky cliffs rose sheer with nothing behind them but sea and sky. All I could see in front of me was the Dead Sea, the same travertine colour as the sky. A haze of either atmosphere or pollution lay over the whole area. It was breathtaking in its aridness: this looked like the entire world. It was a giant, blank canvas and yet it wasn't. There was something hidden and ancient, prehistoric and mythological about it all at once. Even though I could not see one living thing, the whole area felt alive. Now I understood what all the fuss was about. Now I understood how beautiful nothing could be.

We drove back down the mountain, winding past the enormous rock faces that I hadn't noticed on the drive up. After my little stand-off with Hana in the souvenir shop, I had been obsessing about how I behaved and what other people thought of me, both here and at home. Now, on the way back down, I was giving myself a crick in the neck from gaping out the car window. The rocks were oversized, the sky was oversized, the sea was oversized. Without vegetation there was nothing to look at *but* size.

It felt an awful lot like spirituality.

That night I sat and stared out the window of my hotel room and tried to make sense of how I felt. The landscape I had seen that afternoon had left me feeling uneasy in the same way that standing at great heights always does. It's not so much that I am scared that I am going to fall, it's that there's an infinitesimal part of my brain that wants to know what it would feel like to jump. What terrifies me is that one day that tiny spark of curiosity will go mad and throw me over the edge. The landscape of today had filled me with that same terror; a part of me wanted to know what it would feel like to live in a place as empty as that all the time. I imagined my flat back in Australia completely empty. No more hoarding, no more stuff, nothing there but me. And I imagined myself, fearless in the face of regret, fearless in the face of what other people thought of me. I lay on the bed and listened to that little voice deep inside me as it whispered, 'Go on, jump.'

Chapter Sixteen

Early the next morning I arrived at the Jordanian office of the United Nations High Commissioner for Refugees. It was there that I was to meet Dana, my UN contact. I was nervous. My only communication with her had been via email and even then, we had only written to each other twice. I was hoping she hadn't forgotten I was coming. I was also hoping she was a real person. We hadn't been in contact since I had arrived in Jordan.

The UNHCR was housed in a big square building dominating the end of a residential street. There were about fifty people lined up at a booth out the front, mostly men, but a few families as well. There were cement road blocks on either side of the street and half a dozen uniformed guards cradling rifles. On the other side of the road to the main building, a man holding a sign written in Arabic was silently protesting.

I had no idea how I was to get into the building, so I chose a guard who looked a little bit like Orlando Bloom and asked him for directions. He smiled handsomely and pointed me through the road blocks, past a security checkpoint, through a steel door, up a short flight of stairs, through an X-ray bag-check and then through a metal detector, which I again set off to nobody's concern. Directly on the other side, as if the detector served as the doorway, was a small room, and at a desk that took up half the available space sat yet another guard. He gestured for me to show him my passport, then he took it from me and told me to take a seat. I sat down on the only other chair, squashed between the metal detector and a bookcase which held nothing but recharging cradles for walkie-talkies.

As I was making myself comfortable, the guard made a short phone call, then hung up again and looked at me, unsmiling.

'Dana will come at ten o'clock, after her meeting.'

Surrounded by semi-automatic weapons, soldiers and refugees, I felt more relaxed than I had all trip; Dana existed.

I sat and waited. I wished that I had brought a book. I had nothing to do but stare and there wasn't much to look at, just the guard as he did some paperwork. The door behind him was open but all I could see was the bare concrete of a courtyard and, beyond that, a set of double doors. I tried not to fidget. Eventually my guard left and was replaced by another one who, on his way into the room, threw a newspaper past me onto the bookshelf. He didn't even make eye contact. I continued to sit there, invisible and unfazed. After three days, I was slowly becoming inured to the way some of the local men treated me. I'd even managed to accept that it wasn't personal.

On the street below, I could hear a baby grizzling. I was very thirsty. I'd drunk a lot of tea that morning but no water and in this country two litres a day still wasn't enough. It was hot and dry and the office reminded me of my father's workshop when I was a little girl, smelling of grease and dust.

It was then I noticed that the newspaper the guard had dropped was written in English. I thought he was just dumping something he was finished with; instead he was dumping me a favour. I picked it up and was just about to start reading an article about Queen Noor when Dana walked into the room.

She was younger than me, petite with black curly hair. She greeted me with a curt nod and asked me to follow her. More stairs, more doors, more stairs, more doors and, finally, a modest office. Dana went to her desk and pulled an information folder from a pile and handed it to me.

'Today, we will meet some Iraqi refugees at a school. This suits you?'

'Yes.'

'Do you have any questions?'

I was feeling overwhelmed. I had managed to get this far—all the way from Australia—by saying that I was a researcher. Obviously Dana was expecting me to ask pertinent, journalistic-type questions. What I really wanted to ask was: 'Did you know there's a guard out there who looks *exactly* like Orlando Bloom?'

Instead, I asked her about the people I had seen lined up on the street. It turned out that this was where everyone came to register. Nearly all of them were from Iraq.

'Jordan is not a signatory to the UN Convention on Refugees and does not accept asylum seekers as citizens. But our king believes in the brotherhood of the Arab people so if they come, even though they can't be citizens, they can stay. They cannot work, but they can use the schools and hospitals at the rate of a non-insured local. Our job is to assess the people that come here and determine if they are true refugees. If they are, we provide them with resources for many things.'

'Wow, that's generous.'

Dana raised her eyebrows. 'It's not like that in Australia?'

'No, in Australia our government decides if you're a refugee or not. We don't let an independent umpire make the decision for us.'

'And if they decide you are not?'

I looked at my hands, embarrassed. 'They send you away again.'

'Oh. I know that this year you are taking five hundred extra Iraqis, but how many people do you have asking for asylum in Australia?'

'A few thousand. How many refugees do you have in Jordan?'

'Half a million. And we have a population of five million.'

I thought of all those years of the Howard government, when our prime minister had carried on like a housewife in a Looney Tunes cartoon, leaping up and down on a chair, clutching at his skirts and screaming as a couple of hundred malnourished refugees arrived in leaky boats. While he was doing that, Jordan was quietly letting half a million people across its borders. Even though it didn't offer citizenship, at least Jordan didn't turn them away or force them back into the middle of a war zone.

I asked Dana if there were many refugees still coming over the border.

'Not as many as when the war first started but we are registering more and more.'

I was confused. 'Why are they only registering now?'

'Because their money ran out. When these people came here four or five years ago, they thought it was temporary. They believed they would be able to go home again. But as time has passed, all of their savings have disappeared. It is not legal for them to work in Jordan so now they are destitute.' She paused. 'I never thought how much simple things like my clothes meant to me until I started working here.'

We walked out of her office, through the door, down the stairs, through another door, down more stairs, out the double doors, across the courtyard and retrieved my passport from the security guard. Then we went back through the metal detector, past the X-ray machine, down some steps, through the steel doors, past the checkpoint, through the road block and into the back seat of our car. I looked out the window at the protestor, still standing silently where he'd been when I entered the building an hour and a half ago. As our driver started to move off, I asked Dana what his sign said.

'He says that the UN will not help him find a safe place to live. He has been here in Jordan for many years and no one will find him a home. He doesn't understand that the rest of the world will not take every-one. He thinks it is our fault.'

'Does the UN have any figures on how many refugees there are at the moment?'

'There are 11.4 million people registered as refugees.'

It was a staggering figure.

As the protestor with his homemade cardboard sign receded into the distance, the reality of his situation hit me properly: he was on his own in a foreign country with nothing. He was competing with millions and millions of faceless people, all trying to find somewhere safe to live, all in limbo, all slowly watching everything they had ever worked for disappear. And here was I, living in one of the richest countries on earth, with a roof over my head and a good job, gnashing my teeth because I didn't want to throw out an old pair of leg warmers.

'We are travelling to a school bus meeting point run by Save the Children. There are some volunteers there you can speak to.' Dana was dialling a number on her phone and then she was talking to someone to tell them we were on our way.

'The Jordanian government agreed a few years ago to allow the children of refugees to attend school. Refugee children can go to school in Australia?'

Again, I looked at my hands. 'Some of them. Sort of.'

I didn't want to tell her that we held many of our asylum seekers and their kids in jails on an island two and a half thousand kilometres off the coast of Western Australia. It would be like telling her we treated them like vermin.

'Oh. Well, here they can go to school. But Jordan is not a rich country, so organisations like Save the Children cover the cost.' We slowed to a stop and Dana turned to me and smiled.

'Here we are.'

We stepped out of the car. In front of us was a large two-storey building with a verandah running around it. Children wearing backpacks were running around and being herded onto the bus as their parents waved goodbye.

Dana spoke to a woman who nodded and then walked off.

'We will wait here,' Dana said. 'This woman is going to get some of the parents for you. There is a group that come here every day and hand out information about us to the other parents.'

'Like volunteers?'

'Yes. Because there are no organised refugee camps in Jordan, the Iraqis who have come across the border have dispersed into the wider population. They rent apartments in the cheaper suburbs. Many of them do not know that the UNHCR offers assistance with health, legal affairs, counselling and so on. Some parents come here each day to pass on that information.'

Dana and I joined two women and two men sitting in the shade on the edge of a concrete barrier protecting a little garden. I smiled awkwardly. They looked at me expectantly. So did Dana. Goodness knew what these people had seen in Iraq, goodness knew how much they had lost. I was feeling very Western and very privileged. I was waiting for someone to demand, 'What the hell are you looking at, little white girl?'

A man to my right smiled at me. He was middle-aged and wearing a crisp, checked shirt and crease-free trousers. Even though his clothes were worn, they were immaculate.

'Dana, can you ask this gentleman how long he has been in Jordan?' I didn't ask for his name; Dana had already explained that some of these people were still in danger and in hiding.

Dana asked my question in Arabic. He told her six years.

'Umm . . . can you ask him how he came to be here?'

He answered me himself. He had been an officer in the Iraqi army during the war with Iran and, at that time, he was seen as a hero.

'But when the war came from America, many people decided Iran was now our ally. Anyone who fought Iran was now an enemy. Militias hunted us because they thought we should pay for what we had done.'

I was confused. The war with Iran had ended twenty years

ago—dredging it up now made no sense. Maybe this was more to do with the Sunni and Shi'ite tensions we kept hearing about in Australia.

'Is this because of religion? There have always been problems with Sunnis and Shi'ites, haven't there?'

Before the officer could answer, a young man with close-cropped hair, wearing a T-shirt and jeans, said, 'No, that is not the problem. I did not know I was a Sunni until all of this war with America happened. For most of us, this thing was not a problem. I went to the same mosque as the Shi'ites.'

In Australia, we were led to believe that fighting between the Sunni and the Shia populations had always existed and was widespread. These people were telling me that the Western invasion of their country had caused it. I looked back at the army officer.

'So this problem of religion is new? How?'

'My country has fallen apart. People need someone to blame.'

I wasn't sure which made me feel worse: the arbitrary nature of hatred, or the calm way in which this man told me about it. I asked him if it had been hard to leave everything behind.

He replied, 'I stayed after the first attempt on my life, but the second time they came right into my house. I don't know if it was difficult to leave. You don't think when people are shooting at you in your own home, you just run.'

Now, everyone was keen to tell their stories. A middle-aged woman with short brown hair told me her brother hated her because she had married a Sunni. 'Before 2003 we all lived together. None of the children knew who was a Sunni and who was a Shi'ite. It didn't matter to us. Now my own brother tells me that I am a disgrace.' She shrugged. I couldn't imagine telling anyone what she had just told me without bursting into tears.

Another young woman in a red headscarf and jeans told me that she had lived in a Shi'ite part of Iraq all her life, even though she was Sunni. 'It never used to be a problem. Everybody lived side by side until the war. But now everyone hates each other. The militias tried to shoot my husband because he would not join the army.'

The army officer nodded. 'It was compulsory for everyone to serve for one to three years in the army, even the women. The government would punish you or kill you if you did not. Now, the militias want to kill me because I served, they want to kill her husband because he did not.' He paused and smiled at me again. 'You know, I have a brother who lives in Australia. He was given asylum six years ago.'

'Are you hoping to go there too?' I asked.

'I have tried. Three times. Your country says I cannot come.'

No one was blaming me but I felt responsible all the same.

I wanted to ask the group what they missed the most. I didn't expect any of them to say 'my clothes' or 'my jewellery' or 'my car'. I thought they would miss sentimental things: photographs, family heirlooms, their children's baby clothes.

'Out of everything you left behind, what are the things you miss the most?'

It caught me by surprise when they all answered the same way. The middle-aged woman spoke first.

'Stability.'

The army officer and young man nodded and agreed. 'Stability.'

'Stability,' said the woman in the red headscarf. 'Of course! I had a future. My children had a future. Now I have this.' She held out her empty palms to the sky. 'When they shot at my husband, our son was watching. He was three. They shot at my husband and then they set fire to the house. They knew we were still inside it. My son is five now. He still draws pictures of rifles and fire.'

I didn't know what to say.

These people had fled with almost nothing. There was no time to plan an exit strategy, there was no time to pack up crates of belongings and ship them to a nonexistent forwarding address; they arrived in Jordan with less than I had packed for a week-long journey. They'd arrived with nothing other than scars and nightmares and damaged children. They were lucky just to be alive. It put all of my fretting about old postcards and shoes, books and dead flowers into perspective. I felt like I'd finally had some sense knocked into me.

After a restless night's sleep I again met Dana at her office at 10 a.m. This time we drove to a poorer suburb heavily populated by refugees. The closer we got to our destination, the more densely packed in were the buildings and the people. We were on our way to visit a clinic run by Caritas that gave free health checks, referrals and counselling to refugees and impoverished locals. Our driver dropped us by the side of the road and we entered a nondescript multi-storey building wedged between shops and apartments. There were a few people milling out the front. It was so quiet inside that I thought we must have arrived before opening time. We turned into the waiting room and saw the place was full, with standing room only. Everyone was waiting silently. No one took any notice as we moved past them.

We walked up two narrow flights of stairs to meet with one of the doctors who helped run the clinic. Through an open door I saw a teenaged boy with a blank stare hooked up to an ECG machine. Something about him looked wrong, not medically, but psychologically; his eyes were dead. Passing another room with the door wide open, Dana told me that the woman I could see was talking to a gynaecologist. Then we entered a third room where the doctor was still consulting with his patient. We stood there watching them until the consultation finished and the patient got up and left the room. I wondered whether all of this was normal in a Jordanian health clinic or simply the plight of the disenfranchised; perhaps when you were forced to rely on charity you became accustomed to your whole life being laid bare.

We sat down and Dr Jameel, a cheery, enthusiastic man in his early forties, introduced himself. I asked him what were the most common illnesses he saw at the clinic. He ticked them off on his fingers.

'There is a lot of high blood pressure, diabetes and stress-related illnesses, but Iraqi refugees also have a higher incidence of cancer than the Jordanian population. Some say this was caused by depleted uranium used during the war with Iran but really no one knows for sure. All we know is that they have more cancer.'

He told me that the Jordanian government had recently declared that refugees and non-residents could access the national health care system at the same rates as non-insured locals. This meant that for those who could afford it, the health care they needed was always available, irrespective of whether they were a citizen or not. For the rest, Caritas worked hard to find them a place in one of the hospitals that had agreed to take on such cases at a reduced fee.

'For every twenty-five people per week we refer to other hospitals, we can afford to pay for the treatment of the ten most urgent cases. The other fifteen have to pay themselves, or hope that a place becomes available in the future. We are increasing the number that we help every year but it is hard to help everyone.' Dr Jameel smiled at us both and apologised for not being able to stay any longer. He had a lot of patients to see. He took us into a little room off to the side and introduced us to his secretary, who then escorted us back down to the street.

We got into the car and I looked back at the building. There were many more people out the front now, as well as all of those still waiting inside. I couldn't imagine how the clinic would get through so many people in one day. So much about being a refugee rested on luck: luck in getting out of your home country alive, luck in finding somewhere new to shelter, luck in finding a way to earn money and the sheer dumb luck of remaining healthy.

It was lunchtime and Dana had meetings in the afternoon. My two days with her had passed so quickly and now the entire reason for my trip was over. It felt surreal. Tomorrow I would be flying home. I thanked her profusely for giving up so much of her time to help me and she offered to drop me in a part of town where I could find a taxi back to my hotel.

I didn't pay any attention to the scenery out the window as we left the clinic; I was too absorbed by the image of that boy attached to the ECG machine. He had looked irreparably broken.

The car slowed down and stopped at a corner. I smiled at Dana, shook her hand and sincerely thanked her again. Then I stepped out of the vehicle and turned around to discover a world as far from the one I had just left as it was possible to imagine.

I was in Abdoun, the most affluent suburb of Amman, and all around me stood houses of astounding proportions. They were just as white and unadorned as all the others I had seen but they were immaculate and tri-levelled and there was grass (grass!) complementing the elaborately landscaped gardens I glimpsed behind their fences and railings and walls. There were workers tending to the flowers and fountains. There were stained-glass windows and mosaics. I walked downhill for twenty minutes, agog the whole way.

I was hungry and ahead I could see what looked like a little restaurant. I crossed the multi-lane road and walked into a café that may as well have been located in inner-city Melbourne. I had seen nothing like it the whole time I had been here. The glamorous locals seated at the tables in front of me had ordered baguettes, pasta, prawn salads and croissants from an entirely European menu. In less than half an hour the poverty, the uncertainty, the illness and fear of being a refugee were as distant as if I was back in Australia.

I sat down, ordered a cup of tea and a piece of quiche, and looked at the people around me. A television attached to the far wall was mutely showing an international soccer game and pop music wafted from hidden speakers. Everyone was smiling and chatting in air-conditioned comfort, everyone was relaxed and oblivious. The unfairness of the world was slapping me right in the face. How easy it was for us, the lucky ones, to talk about the new dress we had just bought, or how many pairs of shoes we owned, or to complain about how our garages were filled with junk. I stirred my tea and smiled bitterly. How easy it was for us to block out everything else and pretend these things really mattered.

Chapter Seventeen

When I returned to Australia, I attacked my stored-up house of horrors with new vigour. After meeting those refugees in Jordan, I just couldn't look at my stuff in the same way. It was daft to be so obsessed with it all—in fact, it was more than daft, it was a waste of the precious, lucky life that I had been granted. I had a roof over my head, I had friends, I had family, I had everything I needed and I'd been carrying on like I had nothing. Now I had perspective. Now I could see how pointless and irrelevant most of the stuff I had been hoarding really was. And besides, it was winter now and after the heat of the Middle East, the freezing foggy mornings of Melbourne were making my toes shrivel. If I was going to be cooped up inside, then I may as well do something useful.

I'd gone through my wardrobe countless times but I'd always ignored the hard stuff. In fact, one whole third of that wardrobe had not been touched since I'd moved back in. Today, after I'd put on every heater in the house and attempted to warm myself up a little bit, I was going to sort through all of it and this time, instead of flapping around like some daft twit from a Jane Austen novel, I was actually going to do something.

I opened each box, pulled out its contents and dispassionately sorted everything into piles. After four hours I had covered the entire lounge room, some of the kitchen and all of the hallway with little heaps of jewellery, schoolwork, magazines, gifts I had never used and myriad other piles. I stood back and eyed it all objectively. I was not going to play favourites today. I was not going to start with the easiest bits and pieces and ignore the hard ones. Instead, I was going to start with what was directly at my feet and slowly make my way towards the bedroom.

As I worked, I remembered the women and men I had met in Jordan telling me matter-of-factly about running for their lives from men with guns. If I had to leave in a hurry and could only take one or two things with me, what would I take? I looked at the piles I was sorting through. Nothing jumped out at me.

I crawled over to a stack of student newspapers from my university days. I quickly flicked through them, smiling as I read the familiar names of students and friends I had not thought of in years. I didn't need to keep all of this. I found two articles that I had written and one student union election notice containing a spectacularly hideous photograph of me, complete with half-grown-out perm and poorly concealed pimples. I laughed out loud at it. For a brief period of time I had fancied myself as a politician. All hopped up on teenage idealism, I had run for student council, intent on changing the world. My election promises had included the earth-shatteringly original ideas of discounted vegetarian food, cheap movie tickets and free beer. Still laughing, I ripped out the two articles and the election form. A box of newspapers was reduced to three A4 sheets. Every memory from that period of time that I ever wanted to spark, I could do with these few bits of paper. The rest was nothing more than repetition.

Next, I moved to the jewellery. I divided it into childhood, adolescent and adult piles. The adolescent imitation pearl necklaces, multi-hued chandelier earrings and ill-fitting rings that left copper marks on my fingers were easy to throw out; I didn't want to be reminded that I had ever worn such ridiculous stuff, especially the inexplicable pair of Playboy Bunny earrings. The childhood pile was much harder. I couldn't throw out the little bracelet I had worn every day when I was six, likewise the first pair of earrings I had ever bought. I reminded myself that I had shrunk the pile by well over two thirds and moved on. I was not going to waste time flagellating myself for not being able to purge absolutely everything. Now that I had met people who had lived through real suffering, my days of sitting around and wallowing in guilt and self-pity were over.

I worked into the night, only stopping to make fresh cups of tea or put a new CD in the stereo. For the first time in my life as I sorted through knick-knacks, odd socks and cassette tapes that were missing their covers, the 'keeping' pile was significantly smaller than the 'letting go' pile. And for the first time ever, the 'letting go' pile didn't look like a mountain of precious memories about to be destroyed. It simply looked like what it was: a pile of inanimate objects.

Patterns were emerging. I discovered that I didn't need to keep the poster, the script, the notes and the old costume from a university-era play; just one thing, the smallest and most easy to store, would do the job. All of the clothes from my university days brought back the same memories; I only needed to keep one T-shirt to be transported back to that time, not a whole bag full of them. My problem was not that I attached too much importance to objects, it was that I attached the same level of importance to everything. Keeping every single earring I had ever worn meant the ones I really treasured (pearls given to me by my grandmother, a set of little onyx earrings from an aunt) had been dumped in a pile along with a bunch of cheap mood rings and a peace sign I had made myself out of cardboard, glue and dried split peas. Nothing meant anything if I kept it all.

By the end of the week I had reduced four boxes of university memorabilia to one, three boxes of high-school memorabilia to one and my entire childhood was stored in another. As I was packing everything into the university-era box, I realised that the story I had built up of myself from that time was complete fiction. I wasn't nearly as hopeless as I had thought I was. I had started out that way (with terrible hair, agoraphobia and the kind of dress sense that even Helena Bonham Carter would have baulked at), but by the end of four years I was an almost completely different person. It was only after going through those boxes that I remembered I had written two plays that had been produced by the student theatre group, had finally conquered my fear of city people and joined a bunch of clubs and had become confident enough to start auditioning for—and to perform in—a few plays. Not only had I been elected to student council, I had gone on to become president. In short, over that time I had transformed myself from almost-useless to almost-obnoxious. The scared and somewhat ridiculous young woman who spent four years cowering in a dormitory room didn't exist. In front of me—in this box I was now taping shut—was irrefutable proof to the contrary. I smiled. I'd wasted so much time wishing that I could become a strong and independent woman and it turned out I had been her all along, I'd just buried her under a mountain of negativity, depression and rubbish. I didn't need Thomas to look after me—I never had—I'd just lost myself in all the stuff and had thought that he could pull me out again. Now I could see the situation clearly: I had been quite competently looking after myself for years whilst simultaneously telling myself that I wasn't. The contradiction was almost comical: it was as if I'd been sitting in a wading pool, the water barely covering my thighs, and screaming that I was drowning.

I looked at my handiwork. Three boxes in chronological order now held all of my achievements and memories from childhood up until graduation. I had a life story. I made sense. And if I ever started to doubt that, if I ever started to scream that I was drowning again, I could open up these boxes and calm the heck down.

After I'd been home for two weeks, Adam called.

'Are you alive?'

It was a fair question. I had been so absorbed with my clearing out that I had completely ignored not only him, but everyone.

'Yes! Sorry, baby, I'm a bad friend.'

'How was Jordan?'

'It was fine. I got felt up in my armpit.'

'You went all the way to the Middle East for that? Lord, I could have taken you down King Street and got you pregnant for the cost of a Midori and lemonade. Did you ride a camel?'

I giggled. 'No camels. I swam in the Dead Sea though.'

'Oooh! What was it like?'

'Salty.'

I didn't know why I was being so circumspect.

'So, what are you doing now?'

'Nothing much.' Again, I was lying. I was waist-deep in a pile of old pyjamas, trying to sort out if any of them were worth giving to charity or if they constituted something more akin to medical waste.

'Well, let's go get a drink somewhere.'

I hadn't seen Adam in ages and I had been cooped up in the house since I came home. I no doubt had cabin fever and, as a consequence, tonight would probably end with either one or both of us dancing on a table.

Before getting ready to go out, I threw all the pyjamas into a garbage bag, labelled it 'rags' and set it near the door for my next charity-shop run. I was well past the point of over-analysing everything I owned. Somewhere else in the world—probably right at this moment—people were trying to decide whether to stay in their homes and risk getting shot, or leave behind their country and everything they had ever known forever. Dithering over a pair of old pyjama bottoms was making a mockery of what the word 'decision' really meant.

I went into the bathroom to put on some make-up. Every surface now presented an opportunity to de-clutter. As I looked for a lipstick, I realised that my make-up was strewn through two drawers, across the bench and hidden in both cupboards underneath the bathroom basin. Forgetting that I had an appointment to keep, I started clearing out three-year-old mascaras, bottles of solid nail polish and empty talcum powder bottles. I found half a dozen little soaps that had been given to me as gifts when I was still living with my parents. I unwrapped two of them—one for the shower and one for the bathroom—and put the rest on the bench to remind me to use them when the others ran out. I then pulled out at least fifteen half-used body lotions that had also been gifts. If I had put them all on my skin, I would have wound up leaving an oil slick to rival that of the *Exxon Valdez*. I quickly thought of each person who had given one of them to me and silently thanked them. Then I threw the bottles out. When I was done, I was left with one body lotion, one salt scrub, one face moisturiser—one of everything that I actually used. I then spent a good ten minutes admiring my cleaned-out cupboards. I only came back to my senses when Adam sent me a text message saying 'Where the hell are you?' I pulled on my coat and walked out of the house into the wood-smoked winter air.

When I got to the bar, Adam had lined up shots of tequila. He was grinning and waggling a salt shaker at me. We downed the shots then, with eyes stinging and the breath knocked out of us, we ordered a bottle of white wine and found a cosy spot up the back, away from everyone else.

'So have you finished running away now?'

I frowned at him. 'I wasn't running away. And it was your idea that I go to Bali in the first place, remember.'

'Well, yes, but you just kept going after that. Have you spoken to Thomas at all since the whole wedding thing?'

I hadn't thought about Thomas' wedding in over a month. He would have been married by now. 'No,' I said. 'Why would I want to speak to him?'

'Because, Corinne, you never told him that he hurt you. You never mentioned it to him at all. Are you going to avoid this forever?'

I thought about it. I didn't feel like I was avoiding anything. Yes, Thomas had hurt me but I didn't need to tell him that, I couldn't see what it would achieve. And besides, I'd hurt him as well. So much time had passed and so many things had happened in both of our lives that we were never going to find a way to apologise to each other. Maybe we didn't need to anyway; maybe it was more important that we forgave ourselves. I had already done that in Bali; whether he had or had not wasn't anything to do with me. I smiled at Adam in wonder. Six months ago, there was absolutely no way I would have seen things in this light.

I bought us another bottle of wine, sat back down, kissed Adam on the cheek and said, 'There's nothing to sort out with Thomas, honey. Now shut up about it and tell me something interesting.'

He grappled me into a bear hug. 'Now, before I tell you about what I've been doing, why don't you fill me in on the last two weeks of your mysterious life?'

I waved him off. I didn't need to show off about how much stuff I had thrown out. I was a grown-up now, I took care of my own life and didn't look for other people's approval.

'I've just been jet-lagged, that's all. You don't want to hear tedious stories about me readjusting my body clock. For god's sake, Adam, there must be some kind of ridiculous scandal or gossip you can tell me.'

We drank too much wine and, once we had successfully obliterated all our common sense, we moved on to shots of ouzo. The night ended with the pair of us dirty dancing to Kylie Minogue songs in the middle of a bar that didn't have a dance floor.

The next day I woke with a hangover so vicious I thought my brain was going to pour out my nose. I didn't pull myself out of bed until the afternoon and when I finally did and looked around the house, I started to feel a little deflated. Perhaps it was the throbbing of my hangover, but the house looked miserable. There was still so much to do. I had been concentrating on cupboards and wardrobes and spaces that were out of sight. The clutter sitting on the coffee table and benches was all still there and I hadn't even started on the kitchen, not to mention my desk. There were also all the cupboards in the hallway to go through, three bookshelves stuffed with paperwork, trinkets and the occasional book, and I'd completely forgotten about the boot of my car. When I added up all that I still had to do, it didn't feel like I'd done anything.

To cheer myself up, I opened my now roomy wardrobe and stared with pride at the organised clothes, the three neatly stacked boxes and the useful blankets and towels. This was a normal person's wardrobe. I walked into the bathroom and opened all the drawers to admire a normal person's toiletries. Then I looked at myself in the mirror and instantly felt better. Despite the rings under my eyes and unkempt hair that hurt too much to brush today, I was looking at a woman capable of controlling her life, her belongings and her future. I was looking at a woman confronting her demons and slowly but surely achieving the impossible. Some people dream of becoming movie stars or prime ministers or Olympic athletes. I was a hoarder, I dreamed of living unhaunted.

Motivation revived, I dragged out my ladder and spent the afternoon sorting through the top cupboards in the hallway. I had decided that the cluttered surfaces in front of me could wait; it was the monsters hiding in the dark that needed slaying first.

I pulled everything down and determined that none of it would go back up. It was an easy decision to make as none of it was worth keeping: old Christmas wrapping that I was never going to reuse, an ominously titled 'craft box' that held a half-finished piece of knitting, fourteen balls of wool (what I would have given for them when I was eight years old), a bunch of unidentifiable things that had glued themselves to a bottle of PVA and my tennis racquet. I kept the tennis racquet.

I was surprised at how easy all of this had become. Three months ago, I would have sifted through these things—carefully rearranging and smoothing and crooning—then packed it all away again. Now I looked at the mess in front of me and could not see any link between it and the person I had become. If I had ever been a girl who enjoyed half-finished projects, I certainly wasn't now. I had three boxes that held things that I had achieved: plays I had written, shows I had produced, articles I'd had published. That was the stuff that made me proud, that was the stuff I should be reflecting on, not this sticky knotted mess of abandonment and failure. It struck me that the difference between a hoarder and a non-hoarder was not how much of their lives they had failed at, but how many reminders they kept of those failures. I was sure Michelle Obama had not succeeded at everything she had ever put her hand to, but I was equally sure that when she and Barack moved into the White House, she hadn't stashed a bunch of half-finished latch-hook rugs behind the TV cabinet in the Roosevelt Room.

I packed the ladder away again, looked up at the top cupboards and smiled. I was now, officially, a person with empty cupboards. I was okay. I realised this was going to take a long time to do, but I also knew that I *would* get it done; one drawer at a time, one cupboard at a time, one pot or pan at a time, slowly but surely, I would get it done. I felt stronger and more capable than I ever had in my life.

And yet, something still didn't feel right.

Chapter Eighteen

I worked solidly through the winter, pulling things out of cupboards and drawers and returning less and less to them as I went. I was so intent on getting rid of the stuff that I almost became a hermit. I barely left the house and I had invited no one to visit me at home since I'd returned from Jordan. For most of the time, there wouldn't have been room for anyone else anyway. During the clearing out, the place had been so crammed with boxes, clothes and piles everywhere that there was barely enough space for me. But now, after weeks of pillaging and rampaging through my own belongings, apart from a stack of boxes and bags to go to charity, the place looked almost immaculate. There were still a few things that needed attending to, but from the outside, it was clear that I had made headway. More than headway; I was very close to living in a Level Three house.

I rang Adam and demanded he come around straight away. When he arrived, I threw open the front door and grandly stepped aside so he could enjoy the spectacular vista of my one-bedroom flat. He stood in the doorway, hands either side of his face, Macaulay Culkin-style.

'Oh my god! It looks great! Are you sure you live here?' He laughed at his own joke and then suddenly turned serious. 'Corinne, seriously. Are you living here, or have you rented somewhere else for all of your crap and set this place up as a display home?'

'Oh, shut up and get inside.'

I pulled him in, grinning. He walked around slowly, checking out the bookshelves that now held only books and not magazines, scripts, folders and paperwork. He checked under the dining room table and found that the chairs were cleared and could actually be sat upon. He pulled open the little drawers in the coffee table and saw they held nothing except note-pads, pens and a neat stack of takeaway menus.

'You've really done it!' He was staring at me, open-mouthed. I grabbed his hand and dragged him into the bedroom.

'Look in my wardrobe!' I was jumping up and down behind him like an excited six-year-old.

'Wow. This is really impressive. You can actually move things around in here. It looks like a wardrobe you'd see in a magazine—apart from the fact that you have terrible dress sense.'

I slapped him on the shoulder.

We wandered back out to the living area and Adam moved towards the desk. The roll-top was down and he went to lift it. I slammed it shut, almost taking off his fingers.

'Jesus!' He sucked his knuckles. 'What are you hiding in there, Corinne?' He squinted at me suspiciously.

'Nothing.' I was standing in front of the desk, barring his way.

'It doesn't count if all you've done is shove a whole lot of shit under there and *pretended* you've tidied up.' He pushed me aside and flung open the roll-top. A stack of paper slid out and hit the ground. As he bent down to look at it, he noticed the pile stacked up underneath the desk chair.

'What are you doing?'

'Adam, it's just paperwork, it's nothing, really.' I was pleading with him. He was waving a script around.

'This is dated five years ago! What are you *doing*?'

I slid down to the floor next to him. 'I got stuck, Adam. I just stopped being able to do it anymore. It's like I've torn a muscle in my brain and the decision-making part of it has gone into a coma. It's paperwork. It's too hard.'

I wasn't lying; I really did feel like I'd torn a muscle in my brain. I'd been clearing out day after day for weeks and I was exhausted. I'd reached my limit. For the past few days, all I'd done was open cupboards and stare hopelessly at what still needed to be done. The clothes, knick-knacks and books had been easy to get rid of in comparison to all the paperwork. What Adam had found in and under the desk was just the start of it. There were four more shelves stacked high in the hallway. Every time I looked at them I felt faint.

Adam looked at me with sympathy.

'What about that personal organiser you met?'

'What personal organiser?'

'You know, the woman you interviewed.'

I had a weekly radio job and, a few weeks before, I'd had a personal organiser called Lissanne as a guest on the show. She'd given me her card and I'd tucked it away in my purse, never intending to call her. It seemed a bit pathetic to admit that I couldn't tidy up my own house. I avoided Adam's gaze.

'I don't want anyone to see my mess.'

'For god's sake, Corinne, it's her job. And I'm sure she's seen worse. Although,' he considered the script he was holding, 'not much worse. Did you write this?'

That afternoon, after chewing one fingernail down to the quick, I rang Lissanne. She was so capable-sounding on the phone that I instantly felt better.

'Of course I'll come around, Corinne! Now, we won't get everything done in just one session, but we'll tackle your biggest problem area and that will get you going, okay?'

I looked at the desk. 'You really think three hours is enough?'

'More than enough. Trust me.'

Two days later, I led Lissanne into my house. Even though the place looked unrecognisable compared to its former state, I had no idea whether my efforts would meet with the approval of a professional. Lissanne was petite, with groovy glasses, vividly dyed red hair and a penchant for vintage clothing. Before I'd met her, my assumption of a personal organiser had been someone in a corporate suit and white gloves, going around people's houses tut-tutting about dust on skirting boards and pictures of family members in mismatched frames. Lissanne looked at me and smiled.

'What do you want to tackle?'

I pointed towards the desk. I expected this diminutive woman to start berating me at any moment for letting my life get so out of control, but instead she looked at the desk, listed off the order of tasks for clearing it, and then, before I really knew what was happening, we had the drawers out and on the dining table and Lissanne was throwing things into a bin.

'There's a system for getting rid of things,' she said as we worked. 'It's either legitimate paperwork that you need for business reasons, it's something that needs to be actioned, it's truly precious, or,' and here she looked me directly in the eye, 'it's rubbish.' She looked at the stack of old Christmas cards in front of her. 'This is rubbish.'

I had kept every greeting card ever sent to me. I had cards from parents, relatives, best friends, old employers, hairdressers and real estate agents. I had wanted to get rid of them, but it felt sort of evil to throw out other people's best wishes and heartfelt messages. This was what had been holding me back with the paperwork. It wasn't that I couldn't let go of it, it was that I wasn't sure I was allowed to. Now Lissanne was telling me I could. I flicked through the cards and laughingly held one up to Lissanne.

'I guess it says a lot about how little I cook when my local Chinese restaurant sends me a Christmas card from "all their staffs".'

I found one from Thomas, back when he was still signing 'with love'. I shocked myself by realising I was smiling as I looked at it. I had finally got to a point where I could remember our time together with fondness. I kept that one card and we threw out the rest.

'If you find anything else like those cards, you can chuck it without asking first.'

I could hardly believe I had become the kind of person who was capable of saying things like that.

Lissanne and I steadily went through everything, talking very little. I didn't need to Betty-up my possessions anymore and it was surprising how much more quickly we worked if I wasn't babbling away like an insane person. The only time we spoke was for clarification.

'It looks like rubbish to me, but tell me if I'm wrong.' Lissanne handed me what appeared to be an old shopping list. God knows how half this paper had ended up in drawers. I must have simply got to a point where there was so much stuff that I hid it away without even looking at it first, as if I was on autopilot.

Occasionally she would hand me something and I would hesitate. Could I really bring myself to throw out an old stationery set with a picture of Strawberry Shortcake on the front? An aunt had probably given it to me when I was a little girl. Still, there weren't any specific memories attached to it. I was stranded, weighing up the pros and cons of keeping versus tossing. It was bizarre, I had thought I was past all this. Maybe hoarding was an addiction and I was suffering a mild relapse. Perhaps I'd never really fully be over it. Perhaps I'd have to call myself a reformed hoarder forever, not a cured one.

'Corinne, if you don't feel an instant connection to it, it's rubbish.'

Lissanne snapped me out of my reverie. She was right. I would have come to the same conclusion myself, it just would have taken me five times as long to do so. Lissanne picked things up, glanced at them, and then either threw them away or, very occasionally, added them to the keeping pile. I felt nothing but relief. Lissanne moved with a speed it was a pleasure to witness. Then she picked up something that made her stop completely. She read it in its entirety.

'Uh, Corinne, I'm not sure what to do with this one.' Lissanne handed me a crumpled piece of paper, covered in a child's handwriting, avoiding making eye contact with me.

'Perhaps you wrote this when you were little?' Ever the professional, Lissanne was keeping a straight face and I could not see one glimmer of judgement in her eyes. I smoothed out the paper and read:

Dear Bruce Springsteen,
I have blue eyes and brown/blonde hair. I am 23 years old and crazy about you.
I love your music and your body. I long to see you in person. If you get this, please, please answer it.

'Um. I definitely wrote this when I was a kid, Lissanne. Definitely. I would have been twelve.'

'Oh, yes,' she said without looking up, 'I can see that. The writing. Definitely a child's.' She kept sorting.

I wanted to push the point further, to make sure she knew that I really had written it when I was a kid and not as a completely unhinged adult, but I knew if I kept insisting, I'd only make it worse. I reread the note. This was one of those little time-machine moments. I remembered writing this letter as vividly as if I'd done it yesterday.

In 1984 Bruce Springsteen had waggled his hips across my parents' TV singing 'Dancing in the Dark' and I had fallen instantly and hopelessly in love. I had taped the video clip and watched it endlessly, hating Courtney Cox for getting to dance with Bruce when all I could do was watch. I had fantasised about marrying him and planned our wedding down to the last detail: I would wear an enormous ivory wedding gown with puffy sleeves, just like the one Princess Diana wore, and as I walked down the aisle, Clarence Clemons would play 'The Wedding March' on his saxophone. It was going to be an excellent wedding. Bruce would write a new song just for me and instead of the traditional wedding waltz, we'd re-enact the 'Dancing in the Dark' video clip. There would be hot dogs and Golden Gaytimes for the wedding breakfast and on our honeymoon, which was going to be at Dreamworld on the Gold Coast, we would spend long, passionate evenings holed up in our hotel room playing Hungry Hungry Hippos.

I'd agonised over the best way to get in touch with Bruce. This was obviously the biggest hurdle we had to overcome before we got married: we had to meet each other. There was a telephone in my parents' bedroom and one day, when Mum was outside hanging up the washing, I snuck into their room and dialled directory assistance. Even though my mother was outside, I was still petrified that I'd get caught. When the phone operator answered, she spoke so loudly that I nearly jumped out my skin.

'Name?'

I cupped my hand around the receiver and whispered.

'Bruce Springsteen.'

'Who?'

I glanced nervously at the bedroom door. How could this stupid woman not know who Bruce Springsteen was?

'Broooce Springsteeen,' I whispered desperately. 'Sssspringssssteeen.'

I sounded like a snake.

'Oh . . . I'm sorry . . . this is only a local directory. We don't do international calls . . .' And then she hung up. Laughing.

I slammed down the receiver, burning with shame and vowing never to use directory assistance again. That would teach them.

My back-up plan was to draw an elaborate picture of Bruce on an envelope, hoping that would make my meagre piece of fan mail stand out amongst all the millions of other letters he must have been receiving. I laboured over it for days and, in the end, I managed quite a passable likeness. It was only as it was finished and I'd carefully written out the postal address for his record label on the front that I decided it was too childish to send. You didn't meet your future husband by drawing pictures of him; that was the kind of thing an eleven-year-old would do. I was twelve for goodness' sake. I was worldly.

Eventually I hit upon the idea of pretending to be an adult. I have no idea why I chose to be twenty-three years old. Maybe I thought a rounded-off number like twenty-five would sound too contrived. It had obviously not occurred to me that the idea of a twenty-three-year-old telling anyone her age was absurd. I'm surprised I didn't write 'I am 23 years and two months, and this year I want a birthday cake shaped like a bunny'. Presumably the stuff about 'I love your music and your body' was also an attempt to sound adult. I had no brothers growing up, I'd never seen a naked man. I had probably thought Bruce Springsteen running around in the nuddy would look a bit like a Ken doll.

I also don't know what I thought was going to happen if Bruce wrote back. What if he read my letter and thought, 'Why the hell not? Sure, she has the handwriting of a ten-year-old and that stuff about my body is a bit forward, but she definitely sounds keen and she took the time to write . . . maybe I'll fly over to Australia and take her out to Pizza Hut.'

What did I think would happen then? Was I going to pop on a pair of heels and some lipstick and attempt to keep the charade going? Or did I think that when I met him in person my excellent communication skills and mature outlook on life would lead him to overlook not only the age difference, but the My Little Pony T-shirt as well?

I looked at Lissanne. She was busy with the task at hand. I discreetly dropped the letter onto a chair and kept sorting. It was too funny to throw out and I had to show it to Adam. He'd laugh until he cried.

Lissanne was tackling an enormous pile of old call sheets and cast lists from shows that I had worked on. She held one up.

'Do you ever read through these?'

'No.'

'Do you have copies of the performances on tape somewhere?'

'Yes.'

'Then why don't we just keep the first and the last and throw everything else out?'

Why not indeed? In fact, that was an idea I suddenly realised could be applied to an even larger problem. I took Lissanne to the hallway, opened the door and said, 'Maybe we could do the same thing here.'

In front of us was stacked five years' worth of scripts. There would have been over two hundred of them, each thirty pages long, in chronological order, all laboriously hole-punched and filed into ring binders. I had spent hours and hours diligently ordering those papers. They took up an entire metre and a half of shelf space.

'Yes,' said Lissanne. 'First and last. The rest, piff.'

And just like that, I threw away half a decade's worth of memorabilia. I'd been so obsessed with those scripts, thinking that one day they might be worth something, or they might come in handy if I ever needed to refer back to a specific episode of a particular show. But I'd never gone through them; I'd just glanced at them every time I opened the wardrobe and vaguely resented the amount of room they took up. That was the thing about some of my stuff; for some reason I felt that I *had* to keep it, not that I *wanted* to keep it. The scripts were a classic example of that. Now, I was carrying them all out to the recycling bin, relieved to finally have them out of my life.

It took just three hours for Lissanne to cut a swathe through the formerly impenetrable jumble of bills, scripts, notes, newsletters, station-ery, bank statements, receipts and keepsakes strewn over, under and in my desk. Not only was there now room for my laptop and printer, there was even an empty drawer. The speed with which all of this had happened was breathtaking.

In addition to the desk and the shelf, another two boxes had been shrunk down to one document wallet and, outside, one 240-litre wheelie bin was filled with rubbish and the other was full of paper for recycling, thanks mostly to those scripts. Lissanne left with four boxes and two large bags for charity. I'd never eliminated in such bulk or with such speed. I had finally stood on the edge of that precipice and leapt off.

I sat down in my armchair and mentally picked over myself, looking for telltale signs of distress or panic. They didn't seem to be there. In fact, I didn't seem to be feeling anything at all. I rang Adam.

'Hey, sweetpea. Are you all done? How do you feel?'

'I don't know. Sort of like I've had all my hair cut off. I think I'm in shock. Both of my bins are full.' I was sitting still, staring at nothing.

'But you haven't gone downstairs and rescued anything from them, have you?'

'No. And I'm not going to. It's just . . . maybe it was the speed of it.'

'You'll be fine, it's just going to take a little getting used to.'

I picked at an imaginary bit of fluff. 'Yeah.' Then I snapped out of it. 'Hey, can you imagine what those people on those lifestyle shows go through? You know, the ones where some TV presenter invades their house and drags all their stuff out onto the lawn and then throws it all away? The producers should go back again a day later. I'll bet you any-thing they'd find those poor people curled up in the foetal position on the floor.'

'But you're not.'

'No, but that's because I learnt to let go first. If all of this stuff had been wrenched from me before I had sorted myself out mentally, you would now be looking for a psychiatric hospital for me.'

'Who says I'm not anyway?'

I laughed. 'I love you, Adam.'

'Love you too, baby. Mwah.'

I looked around my flat. There was so little left to do now. One drawer here, half a box there and it would all be over. I couldn't believe it. I was so close to achieving my dream of living unburdened.

And yet, like before, something still didn't feel right.

I got up from the armchair and walked carefully around the apartment, staring my things in the face. There was something in here that was haunting me, I could feel it. I checked out my bookcases. Nothing in there made me feel guilty or miserable. Nothing on my desk made me feel bad either. I walked past the framed poster that Thomas had given me and into the bedroom. I searched under the bed. Nothing. I opened the side of the wardrobe in which I kept my clothes. Nothing. I was just about to close it again when the edge of something caught my eye. It was the mirror Thomas had given me. After the painful way things had ended, I had stashed it in the wardrobe, not wanting to see it anymore.

Now I knew what the problem was.

I went back out to the lounge room. Here was the framed poster he had given me, here was a limited-edition book, a novelty pencil and an atlas, here was a collection of wine from a trip we had taken together, here were the kitchen knives and screwdriver set that had belonged to him and that he'd given me when I moved out on him.

Adam was right after all; I hadn't moved on. I looked around the house again. Thomas was everywhere. Guilt was everywhere. Some of the things he'd given me when we were still together, many of them he'd given me after I'd left him. This was what was haunting me, no doubt about it. I sat down in the armchair again and allowed myself to cry, just a little bit;

Thomas had been my friend and I had loved him. The ending of our time together deserved to be mourned properly.

Then I stood up, gathered everything he had given me into a pile, and started deciding who was going to get what. Finally, I was ready to let go.

Part 5
When It Was Done

Chapter Nineteen

'Sold! To the woman sitting in the gutter.'

Is that real estate agent looking at me? I think he is. I'm definitely sitting in a gutter. I definitely put up my hand when he said, 'Are there any other offers?'

It appears that I've just bought a house.

I nodded casually to the crowd, stood up, brushed myself off and walked into the little two-storey brick cottage that I apparently now owned. The real estate agent smiled at me expectantly. He was holding out a pen. I really hadn't meant to do this, I was just passing by. I'd only seen the interior twenty minutes before and I'd only spent ten minutes looking through it. I didn't recall seeing a bathroom. I pushed my sunglasses up to the top of my head, smoothed down the cruddy old tracksuit pants I was wearing and took the pen from the immaculately suited man in front of me.

'Thanks. Just one thing before I sign . . . does it have a toilet?'

The real estate agent's smile faltered.

For two months I had been unsuccessfully house-hunting. After I had packed up the last remaining items Thomas had given me, I had spent a delightful few days passing them on to friends. My cousin received the antique mirror, another friend was given the framed poster and I invited myself to Adam's house for dinner and we shared an incredible bottle of deep red wine that I had bought with Thomas on a holiday when we were still together. Everyone was delighted and surprised by the things I had given them, and I was delighted and surprised to discover how much fun it was to give them away.

And yet, unbelievably, something was *still* wrong. There were three empty shelves in my cupboards, two empty drawers in my desk, I could easily sift through my clothes and there was nothing under the bed. My house was almost unrecognisable, I had conquered my stuff. So why was there still this oppressive feeling every time I unlocked the door and stepped into my flat? I wondered this aloud to Adam one afternoon as we sat in his backyard, trying desperately to soak up the feeble sunbeams of early spring, eating fish and chips and fighting over the sauce bottle.

'I don't know what's wrong. I've virtually got everything under control but I'm still having nightmares. I still feel like there's something breathing down my neck waiting to lunge out and attack me.'

Adam licked his fingers. 'Where do you live?'

'Don't be an idiot, Adam, you know where I live.'

'No, *where* do you live?'

I rolled my eyes. 'In a *flat*.'

'That . . .' Adam was rolling his hands at me, encouraging me to finish his sentence.

'. . . has four walls and a roof. Where the hell are you going with this?'

'Okay, we'll start again. Where you do you live now?'

I sighed. There was no point in arguing with him when he was like this. 'I live in a one-bedroom flat over there.' I waved over the fence in the vague direction of my place.

'And where did you live before that?'

'In a hellhole on the edge of reality.'

'And before that?'

'In the same little flat I'm in now, but with my ex-boyfriend . . . oh my GOD!'

Adam laughed hysterically as I stared at him, open-mouthed with horror.

'I'm hoarding a *flat*? Oh my GOD!'

I started flapping my hands like they were covered in something disgusting.

'I've got to get out, I've got to get out. Why didn't you tell me?'

'Would you have listened?'

I stopped flapping. 'No, I wouldn't have. I would have offered you a whole lot of excuses. I would have been in complete denial.'

'And now?'

'And now I am moving out. As soon as I can.'

Initially I had only wanted to rent something new. I wanted a little house with two bedrooms not because I wanted space for storage but because I wanted a room to turn into an office. I also liked the idea of having a little backyard. This time, it would be fun to find somewhere new: I wasn't constrained by ridiculous needs for excessive storage.

I pored over my budget and figured out I could afford to pay one third more in rent than I was currently paying. What I had failed to notice while I was happily sequestered away in my little flat—enjoying the same rental rates I had been shelling out since the time Thomas and I had shared the place—was that the market had gone completely crazy. While I had been living in fairyland, a housing shortage had been growing around me. Renters had become so desperate they were bidding for properties. People were offering twelve months' rent in advance, they were signing over their firstborn children and proffering their kidneys in lieu of bond money. There were so many people and so few houses that everyone had lost their minds, including the landlords. Places far worse than the hellhole were now raking in the kind of money I would have associated with a penthouse suite that came complete with a live-in high-class hooker.

I spent every weekend for a month wandering through slums, enduring the teenaged real estate agents who stood out the front, imperiously waving clipboards and acting like door bitches at exclusive nightclubs. I half expected to have to pay a cover charge just to cross the threshold. Every house I walked into Ate A Dick. There were places next to building sites and factories, and places that smelt of mildew and rotting fruit. They often had no heating or cooling and, in one, a non-working wood stove in what appeared to be a bedroom was described to me as a 'rustic kitchen'. Another place, which was advertised as having a second bedroom, was actually referring to the space between the ceiling and the roof. They'd put a ladder up to the access hole and I supposed you saved on bedding by sleeping on the insulation batts. I was back in the same situation as when I'd left Thomas.

I had no desire to repeat history. This time when I left, I was going to leave for something better, and if I was going to spend an obscene amount of money on a place to live, I decided, then I may as well buy something. That way I could hammer in as many picture hooks as I liked, I could paint the walls, put up shelves and dig up the garden. I was also sure I had read somewhere that if you were a landowner and the next-door neighbours held a party that went until dawn, you were allowed to pour burning pitch over their heads.

I sat down with a calculator. Once I pooled all my savings and emptied my term deposit, I would have a relatively substantial deposit. Now I was getting excited. I started fantasising about Victorian terraces with enormous backyards, entrance halls and bay windows. I imagined having a study with wall-to-ceiling bookshelves, chesterfield lounge suites and a hand-hewn dining-room table. There would be a stove with room for a fish kettle (whatever that was), a stainless-steel fridge that dispensed ice cubes, and a claw-foot bath in the oversized bathroom.

I started looking in my suburb and it became apparent within five minutes that I couldn't afford anything close to that. If I was lucky I might manage an apartment slightly bigger than what I was renting now and, if I was even luckier, it might be an apartment with windows.

I adjusted my expectations.

A week later, I found a place in a block of flats I thought I could live in. The next-door neighbours appeared to be normal and the building didn't smell like anyone was cooking up drugs in their kitchen. There were windows and new carpet, there were built-ins in the two bedrooms and a little balcony overlooking the busy street below. It even had city views if you climbed up on the kitchen island, stood on tiptoes and employed a telescope. The auction was in two weeks' time. I quickly arranged a building and pest inspection, gathered all the paperwork together and gave it to a conveyancer to check over. Everything seemed fine. The flat was even advertised at well below what I could afford to pay. I allowed myself to get a little bit excited.

My only problem was the auction. I had never bid on anything before, not even at a charity event. Buying lotto tickets scared me. There was no way I could risk doing this myself; I knew I would panic and forget to put my hand up even once. Then, luckily, I was introduced to a friend of a friend. His name was Julian and he had bought two houses for himself and had bid on behalf of nearly everyone else he knew. He seemed friendly enough and, although he had a disconcerting habit of looking away whenever he was speaking to me, he knew a dizzying amount about the auction process. If there was such a thing as an auction nerd, I had found it.

On the morning the apartment was to be sold, I sat a little further up the road at a café with my friends Gerard and Katharine. My mobile phone and a plate of uneaten poached eggs sat in front of me. Julian told me he would only call if things got tight and he needed me to decide on any further bids. Adam rang from his holiday in Sydney to ask me how the auction was going and I almost yelled at him to get off the phone and stop clogging the line. He laughed and hung up. Then the phone rang again. Julian sounded excited.

'You hear that?' In the background I could hear the auctioneer calling out numbers two hundred thousand above the advertised price. That could not possibly be right. I frowned.

'Where are you, Julian? Please don't tell me you went to the wrong auction.'

'Nup. I'm here. It's gone crazy.'

It felt like I had been done an injustice. Someone—definitely not me—was responsible for needlessly getting my hopes up.

'That's ridiculous. Who would pay that much for a flat?'

'It's two guys in suits. I think it's less about the property and more about the size of their dicks. The rest of us are just standing back and watching.'

I listened to the rest of the auction by phone. In the end, the little apartment I thought would be mine went for the price of the mansions I knew I could never afford. I stared glumly at the eggs congealing on the plate in front of me.

'Looks like there's a property boom on!' Julian sounded thrilled.

My suburb was now way out of my reach.

'Not to worry, you can always try again a little further out.' Julian hung up before I had a chance to start swearing at him.

I didn't want to try 'a little further out', I wanted to live here where I knew everyone. I knew Steve who ran the fruit and vegetable shop, Alex who owned the cocktail bar, Dolores who owned the deli and Sebastian at the flower shop where I bought bunches of jonquils I didn't want because he was cute and had an accent. Gerard lived in the next street along from me. Katharine lived a ten-minute walk away. My friend Fahey and her two hilarious children were my regular Monday lunch date. Adam was only two tram stops from my house. I had found a little community within a big city and I didn't want to leave it. Those years in the hellhole, far from my friends and completely on my own, were still painfully vivid. As nice as owning my own place would be, it wasn't worth losing everything that mattered to own one thing that might.

However, the reality was undeniable: I couldn't afford to rent and I couldn't afford to buy in this suburb. My only other option was to stay where I was, living in the same flat I had shared with my ex-boyfriend and lying in bed at night feeling him seeping out of the walls. I shuddered at the thought.

I reluctantly started looking in a suburb a ten-minute drive further north. I drove out to look around the area and, to my surprise, I didn't mind it too much. The streets were lined with blossoming trees, all the houses had rosebushes out the front and I didn't see one abandoned shopping trolley. And everything was quiet. I had lived surrounded by noise for so long that I'd forgotten that most people don't live in places where they need earplugs just to get a good night's sleep. I bought a newspaper and started circling likely properties.

That weekend, on my first round of open houses, I found a place that I instantly loved. It was a beautiful two-bedroom Edwardian, with a climbing rose over the front verandah and a little study built on the lawn out the back. It had ducted heating and polished floorboards and a big tree in the yard. The front bedroom had an open fireplace and was filled with sunshine. I wanted to live here more than I had ever wanted to live anywhere. Adam was with me and I turned to him to ask what he thought of the place. He was leaning against the bedroom door with his eyes closed.

'Adam!'

He jumped awake. 'What, I'm here! Oh, yes, lovely. Hmmm.'

The day before, Adam had agreed to come house-hunting with me. He had then put on his best clothes and headed out to a friend's birthday party. When the last bar closed at 10 a.m. that morning, he walked out of it and straight to my place. He looked like a junkie and smelt like he had taken a nap on a toilet floor.

Now he was leaning against the doorframe, half asleep and trying to look apologetic.

'Sorry, I probably shouldn't have come with you today. I think I smell like a department-store Santa.'

I rolled my eyes and kept looking. People do house inspections in the same way they walk through art galleries. They stand thoughtfully in each room, murmuring *sotto voce* to their partners, their forefingers on their chins and glossy brochures in their hands. They don't show emotion and they don't reveal what they really think of the place. Adam took a different approach. We had already looked through two other houses that morning and he had caused a scene in both. At the first, he had walked into a house that had obviously once belonged to an old man and announced loudly, 'Oh, luv, you can't buy this! Someone's grandad carked it in here!' We left immediately.

The second place we visited was a brand-new townhouse. Like so many others I had visited, it was mass-designed, ostentatious and at the same time cramped, impractical and devoid of personality. Someone had decided to lay a swirling green carpet in the living area, presumably in an attempt to give the place some kind of character. Looking at it gave me vertigo. Adam clutched at his head, loudly proclaimed, 'This carpet is vomit,' and staggered dramatically back out the front door. I quickly followed, avoiding the disapproving gaze of the real estate agent.

When we got to the car I looked at him as sternly as I could.

'Adam, we are inspecting houses, we are not touring a one-man show called "Attack of the Crazy Drunk Man". Pull yourself together or I'm leaving you in the car.'

He grinned lazily and looked mostly in my direction. 'Okay, sweetpea.

I'll behave. Unless the next house is really shit and then I can't be held responsible.'

Thankfully, when we walked into the little Edwardian he kept his mouth shut and, apart from the odour and the swaying, he passed for almost normal. I walked through the whole house slowly and thoughtfully, trying to hide my excitement. It was gorgeous; there was even a cat flap in the back door. I didn't own a cat but if I moved here, I would definitely get one. I wanted this house.

On the way out, I asked the real estate agent a couple of questions about the price of other properties in the area and how much the rates were. In return, he asked me if I would be buying on my own. I looked at him, puzzled. I couldn't see the relevance of the question until Adam answered, 'Oh I'm not living here with her, I'm just her drunk friend.' The agent looked relieved.

Once again, I passed on all the details to my conveyancer, organised the building inspection and rang Julian to ask him if he was willing to try his hand at another auction. He told me he was going to be out of town. Now I was stuck. Even if I had been game enough to do the bidding myself, I wasn't going to be here either. I had a job in Darwin and there was no way I could cancel with only a week's notice. I sat down at my desk and tried to nut out a solution. Then I searched the internet looking for a buyer's advocate. I found one called John. We met over coffee and he was so earnest and enthusiastic that I liked him instantly. Still, it felt wrong sending a stranger to handle such a big decision, so I asked my sister Wendy to go along as well.

'I don't have to bid, do I? You know I'll go crazy and either buy the house for too much money or hit whoever wins.'

'No! Good grief. John will be there, you just have to hand over my signed cheque as a deposit if I get it. Please don't hit anyone.'

Again, I felt a bit excited. Thanks to being a little further out of town, this house was way below my limit. Even if things went crazy, I would still be in the competition.

The day of the auction came and I sat in a hotel room thousands of kilometres away, staring at my phone, waiting for John to call and tell me whether I'd got the house or not. Like Julian, he was only going to ring if it was getting close to my price and the bidding was still heated.

The phone rang.

It was Wendy. 'Corinne, can you go another ten thousand?'

I looked at the ceiling.

'Corinne?'

I was dithering. That would put me outside my limit.

'Corinne!'

'Oh god, okay, just ten.'

'Too late, it's just gone up another fifty. Some chick just won it. She's jumping up and down. Do you want me to hit her?'

'No!'

I hung up and threw out the brochure of the pretty little house that I'd had sitting on my lap for the last hour. I couldn't afford to live where I wanted, I couldn't afford to live further out and I couldn't afford to rent something decent. At this rate, I was going to have to move into a wheelie bin next door to a brothel.

When I got back to Melbourne, Adam met me at the airport.

'You'll find something, honey. People spend years trying to find a house.'

'Thanks, that helps a lot.'

He laughed. 'Look, maybe you should lower your expectations. Find something in a bad part of town, or something run down. It's a better option than having to move further and further out. If you keep trying to find this imaginary perfect house you'll be so far out of the city that you'll be switching time zones every time you come back to visit.'

Perhaps he was right. I'd lived in a hovel once before, maybe I could do it again. At least this time I would be closer to my friends and I could always renovate and get a guard dog. I started looking in my suburb again, but this time I focused on the places where there was a drug problem, high crime, or a footballer living next door.

The next Saturday, before I started inspecting the run of local dumps I had found in my price bracket, I took myself out for breakfast. I was about to drag myself through four rundown houses: one that was situated next to an industrial estate, one that was partly demolished, one that was ominously described as 'needing work' and another that was beside a power plant that visibly shimmered with electromagnetism. Presumably the owners of that house had moved somewhere bigger to accommodate their ever-growing tumours. The hellhole was starting to look like a real estate gem. I needed some cheering up. I ordered eggs, bacon, hash browns, mushrooms, spinach, orange juice and hot chocolate, figuring if I'd missed anything on the menu I could always order seconds. I flicked through the paper as I waited for it all to arrive. John had told me there was a little house in my price bracket up for auction that day and I should swing by to see what it went for. I had looked it up that morning on the internet. It was recently renovated and in a street where houses often went for more than a million dollars. I scoffed at their ridiculously low asking price. I knew too much about auctions now to be fooled by that kind of rubbish. Still, it was going to be sold before my first inspection. There was no harm in dropping by and watching the drama unfold.

I arrived at the house early and wandered through it to kill some time. As soon as I stepped inside I wished I hadn't. The house was perfect, a tiny two-bedroomer, just big enough for one person who wanted an office. There were skylights and purpose-built shelves tucked under the stairs. There was even a small courtyard out the back. I went out the front again and waited around, thinking I might not watch the auction after all. It would be too depressing to watch it sell for a thousand-million more dollars than I could afford.

As I stood there daydreaming I realised that the auctioneer had already started to go through the formal proceedings. I was standing right beside him and I wasn't dressed for the occasion. My unwashed hair was pulled back in a bun, I was wearing my worst tracksuit pants and sneakers, and there were at least fifty people staring in my direction. I'd dressed appropriately enough for inspecting slums; I hadn't dressed at all suitably for a flashy auction on a flashy street. I panicked and immediately sat down where I was, which happened to be the edge of the gutter, at the auctioneer's feet. At the time, it felt inconspicuous.

The bidding started at the advertised price and no one raised their hand. I put my arms around my knees and leant back a little, getting comfortable. This always happened at auctions. Things started off slowly and then all of a sudden there would be three or four people bidding aggressively, eyeing each other off, talking on their mobile phones and whispering frantically behind their hands. I looked around the crowd, trying to pick who those likely bidders would be. Time went by. And by. The auctioneer was about to pass in the property when a middle-aged man finally put up his hand. Another ten thousand dollars had been added to the price. Yet again there were no other bids. The auctioneer started to count down the first call, the second call and then, just as he was about to call out the third and final, I stuck up my hand and yelled 'Ten!'

Had I really just done that? Apparently I had. I'd just bid at an auction. I felt like I'd done the most powerful thing in the world and, now that I'd done it once, I didn't seem able to stop. A red haze passed over me and before the other man finished calling out his next bid, I beat his offer with another ten thousand. I was well within my range; this little house was insanely underpriced. We kept going back and forth and I never let the other person get out a full bid before I interrupted him with mine. I'd never realised how aggressive I could be—that trip to the Middle East must have done me some good. I was having an enormous amount of fun. Then the other man pulled out. The bid was with me. The auctioneer looked around the group.

'Are there any more bids at this moment, ladies and gentlemen?'

Everyone stayed silent.

'Okay. I'll just go inside and ask the owners if the property is on the market.'

Now I had a moment to think. If no one else made a bid, I was about to buy a house. I shook the idea out of my head. I had been to a bunch of auctions around this area now, trying to get a feel for the process, and this always happened. People like me splashed around in the puddles of our meagre savings until we ran out of cash, then the serious bidders swept in and, before you knew it, the property you thought was yours was now a hundred thousand dollars beyond your grasp.

'Ladies and gentlemen, are there any further bids?'

No one moved.

'Going once.'

This always, *always* happened. They waited until the last moment. I didn't mind, I'd never expected to actually buy the house, I'd only been playing.

'Going twice. Are there any more bids? Ladies and gentlemen, you won't get a bigger bargain on this street any time soon, I assure you.'

I was getting impatient now and wished that whoever was going to put in the next bid would stop being so dramatic and just get on with it.

'Ladies and gentlemen, as soon as this brochure hits my hand, the property will be sold. Going once, going twice . . .'

The blood drained from my head and pooled in my feet.

Slap!

'Sold. To the lady sitting in the gutter.'

Everyone looked at me. I stood up slowly, thanking God that I was wearing sunglasses and no one on the street could see the terror in my eyes. I'd been wandering past. I'd been on my way to look at places I could afford. I wasn't supposed to be here.

Inside the house, the owners and their parents were opening a bottle of champagne and I accepted a glass blindly. I had so much adrenalin coursing through my veins that I could have knocked back the entire bottle and still remained sober.

The real estate agent smiled and held out his pen.

'Shall we sign the documents?'

I grabbed his sleeve and started babbling.

'Idon'trememberseeingthehousewhat'sgoingonI'veneverbidatanauctionbeforeisthereatoilet? Is there a toilet?'

The real estate agent recoiled slightly. From his point of view, he was looking at a woman who had strolled up to a public sale in her tracksuit pants, plonked herself down in the gutter and proceeded to aggressively outbid the only other person interested. Now it seemed all that might have been a mistake. Perhaps all she'd wanted was to use the facilities.

I took a deep breath and asked if I could look around again, explaining that I'd only briefly looked through the place just before the auction started. I climbed the stairs. Yes, here were the two bedrooms. My bedrooms. I walked down again. Here was my stove. Here was my bath and shower and, thankfully, toilet. Here was my courtyard. I'd bought a house!

I had another glass of champagne and signed all the paperwork. An elderly lady, who I assumed was the grandmother of one of the owners, winked at me and said, 'It's a great party house.' I smiled at her and told her that was wonderful as I loved entertaining. It was a complete lie. I didn't know whether I liked entertaining or not. I'd never lived anywhere I could fit people.

'Of course, on the downside,' said the grandmother, 'there's a terrible lack of storage. Apart from what's in the bedrooms and kitchen, there's only this.' She was pointing to the one cupboard and shelving under the stairs.

I smiled at her and held out my glass for a refill. 'That won't be a problem.'

Chapter Twenty

Once the initial excitement over buying a house wore off, I started to worry. Would all of my stuff fit inside it? I surveyed my apartment, trying to imagine everything packed into the other wardrobes and drawers, and couldn't make up my mind. Instead, I decided it was better to be safe than sorry.

It was time for another cull.

I thought hard. Lissanne and I had eliminated a staggering amount from my desk in a very short time; there were probably similar opportunities to be found everywhere else. I went into the bathroom and checked the cupboards. Nope. I'd already been through here and all that was left were the lotions and potions that I actually used. I picked up some clothes lying on the bathmat, walked back out again and opened the door to the European laundry. Sitting on top of the washing basket was an inflatable exercise ball that I never used. Every time I wanted to put something in, I had to lift the ball up with my free arm, steady it with my head and quickly throw the washing into the basket underneath it. I'd been doing this for three years. I shook my head in disbelief at how daft I was. How, after all that I had thrown out, had I missed something so big? I must have had some sort of hoarder's blindness. I pulled it out, released its valve and watched it shrink as the air hissed out. When it got to the point where there was not enough internal pressure left to force out the remaining air, I lay down on it and rolled back and forth to squeeze it flat. It was the most exercise I'd ever done on the thing.

Next, I stood back and stared at my linen cupboard. It was crammed full of towels, sheets, pillow cases and face cloths. I hadn't gone through any of it. I only used about a third of what was in there. There were sheets for a single bed that I had slept in when I'd first moved to Melbourne. There were pillow cases old enough to qualify for carbon dating. I even had one towel I'd bought in a charity shop because it reminded me of when I was little. In effect, I was storing someone else's childhood in my wardrobe. That was probably the kind of thing serial killers did. I kept the best linen and fluffiest towels and put the rest on the start of another pile for charity.

Then I remembered that not all of the linen was stored here, some of it was in a chest at the end of my bed and there was another little pile in the wardrobe. This was a hoarder's trick I had completely forgotten about: if someone came around and only looked in the wardrobe, the neat little stack of towels and face cloths resting there looked perfectly normal. Likewise, if a visitor only looked in the chest at the foot of my bed, or only in my linen cupboard, then there didn't appear to be a problem. But when you added it all together (as even I had never done) it looked like I had robbed a Kmart. When I located them all and counted them, I discovered I owned thirty-two face washers. No wonder it had taken so long for me to realise how big my hoarding problem was—I'd been hiding my stuff from myself.

I went over the entire house like I was a detective, inspecting every single space I could think of. I filled another two garbage bags with linen, clothes, books and the exercise ball. There was now not one cupboard, one box, one drawer, chest or basket that had not been thoroughly examined and purged.

I was done. I was really and truly done.

And yet, I didn't feel a sense of elation or achievement. I huffed in exasperation. I had always imagined this moment would be stupendous, that I'd be standing on a mountain top like Julie Andrews, spinning in circles and warbling some celebratory tune. Instead, I felt vaguely dissatisfied.

I sat down and tried to work out how much stuff I thought I had abolished from my life. This, I thought, would give me that longed-for sense of accomplishment. I stretched my memory back a year, to the day Adam and I had done our big charity shop run, the same day we had found out about the Bastard Man's death. I counted everything I could remember discarding from that point on: I had given piles of stuff to charity, to other people and to the rubbish bin. I sat down with a notepad and pen and wrote it all down. There was *Le Marchepied*, bags and bags of old clothes, books and CDs, numerous knick-knacks and ornaments, all the Thomas stuff, and there was probably enough paperwork, magazines and newspapers to papier mâché an elephant. When I added it all up, I estimated I had eliminated the equivalent of twenty moving boxes. Twenty moving boxes!

I looked around the apartment. It was still six weeks until settlement on the new place but I couldn't bear the wait; I wanted to know how many boxes it would take to pack everything that was left. I put on my most comfortable clothes, slid the Jackson Five into the stereo and started packing.

For the first time in my life, getting ready to move was not only easy, it was fun. Once upon a time, if I'd had skeletons in my closet, I would have had to move three old doonas, a moth-eaten blanket and a taffeta ballgown from the mid-eighties just to get a glimpse of their bony faces. Now, not only the stuff was gone, but the skeletons as well. There wasn't a single psychological booby-trap waiting to spring out at me. I danced around the house, wrapping vases and crockery in my remaining towels and sheets. I packed up photo frames and prints, cooking utensils, books, underwear, socks, jewellery, shoes, belts, the lot. Everything I pulled out was either useful or had tangible value. It was like I'd put all of my possessions in a giant gold-pan and sifted away the dirt.

In two days I was finished. I counted the number of boxes it had taken me to pack, then punched the air and whooped. There were twenty-four of them. If I'd already rid myself of twenty boxes, that meant I'd nearly halved my worldly possessions. It was an incredible feeling. I spun around the lounge room in circles, singing off key and generally behaving like an idiot.

A little less than a year ago, I'd been standing in my bedroom surrounded by broken glass, crying my eyes out, convinced that I was useless and worthless. Since then I'd travelled halfway around the world, met incredible people, learnt to stand up for myself and bought a house. It was hard to believe that I'd ever thought I was unable to cope on my own.

I admired the neat stack of twenty-four boxes again. I'd never felt so good about being brought down to size.

A week later I was sitting on Adam's kitchen bench, swinging my legs back and forth and showing off.

'What do you mean you've finished packing?' Adam was standing at the stove, stirring something that he insisted was going to be a roux. I had expected him to be overcome with admiration when I told him that five weeks out from settlement on my new house I was living with just one set of sheets and one bath towel. I was expecting the usual 'Good girl!', which he said in the same way most people praised a dog that had finally learnt how to sit on command.

'How are you living? What are you washing with? Why did you pack away your towels?' Maybe he was just miffed because I hadn't asked him to help.

'I didn't pack the towels on purpose, I just needed them to put around the breakables. I kept out some of my clothes and my toiletries.'

He made some kind of sniffing noise and kept stirring.

'When are we going shopping then?'

I stared at him in amazement.

'I don't need to buy anything, Adam, I'm a reformed hoarder. If I was an alcoholic would you be offering me a drink?'

'So you're going to drag the old chair of Thomas' and the old coffee table of Thomas' and the old rug of Thomas' and you're going to set them all up in your new house, are you? You're going to keep dragging him around with you? Good girrrrrl.'

There was a buzzing in my ears. I couldn't believe I still had stuff that belonged to Thomas. How had I missed that? Perhaps I was suffering from hoarder's blindness again. It hadn't occurred to me that those things had originally belonged to him—in fact, they almost seemed to belong to the apartment, not to Thomas—that was the only reason I could fathom for having kept such obvious reminders of him in the house. Not willing to keep those things for even a second longer, I pulled out my mobile phone, rang the Brotherhood of St Laurence and arranged a home pick-up to take the furniture away the next day.

'Done!' I smiled smugly.

'You realise that means you're going to be living without a coffee table for the next month and a half?'

I stopped swinging my legs. ' . . . yes.' I faltered. 'I did it on purpose.'

For the next five weeks I ate my dinner off my lap and fantasised about how I was going to set up the new place: all my CDs and DVDs would go in the drawers beneath the stairs; I no longer needed the big entertainment unit I had stored them in because I'd given half of them away. The towels would fit in the little space below the wash basin in the bathroom; they didn't need a whole shelf in a wardrobe anymore. The cupboard downstairs would hold my ladder, brooms, suitcases and other big things. Everything else would fit in the built-ins in the two bedrooms. I clapped my hands excitedly and counted down the days until I left this apartment and its ghosts behind forever.

On a warm day in late summer I sat out on the balcony, killing time until the removalists arrived. I wandered around aimlessly, picking buds off the bougainvillea spilling over the railings and scuffing little bits of dirt through the cracks in the decking. Normally I spent the morning of a move cramming my car with 'special things' that I was scared the removalists might break. This time, I'd carefully placed a few delicate vases and framed photos in the boot and that was all. I was done. I looked at my watch. I even had enough time spare to make one final trip to the op shop.

This was a job I had been saving for a few days. It was something that I'd wanted to do on my last day in this flat, if I had enough time, to really signify that I was ending one thing and beginning another. I'd received a flyer in the mail earlier in the week from the Brotherhood of St Laurence. They were starting up a second-hand bookstore to help fund their work. It was perfect timing: I had one more possession that needed to go.

I drove to the Brotherhood, went inside and handed over the Bastard Man's book. Someone else could read it now. That was the best legacy I could leave on his behalf: he could bring someone else joy. I drove back home with tears in my eyes, laughing at my sentimentality.

When the removalists arrived, I calmly stood back and watched them carry everything out to the van. I didn't feel embarrassed about the amount of belongings I had, I wasn't still packing madly and I wasn't on the verge of a nervous breakdown and acting like I might throw myself down the stairs at any moment.

When we arrived at the new house, the hardest thing we had to do was carry my bed up the staircase to the second level. There were no broken things to be handled carefully through the front door, no half-dead pot plants or ancient electrical equipment and no heavy bags of old clothes, skulking around like would-be criminals.

By mid-afternoon I was standing in the middle of my own house, furniture in all the right places and boxes in the right rooms ready to be unpacked. I sat down on the edge of the step leading from the kitchen to the lounge and looked around. It was still hard to believe I owned this place.

It took me less than a week to unpack properly. And amazingly, along the way, more stuff went: clothes, books, linen, trinkets. I'd only been in my new place a few days and already I was leaving bits of furniture out the front with signs saying 'free to good home'.

When I was finished, everything had a place and there was even room to spare. I had turned into the kind of person who could live comfortably without much storage. It was as if I had sprouted wings and learnt how to fly.

About five of the boxes I moved were filled with memorabilia and ephemera. They were labelled and stacked neatly in the wardrobe in the study, next to my tax documents and photo albums. Five boxes may still have been a lot to some people, but it was only one-fifth of what I had been hoarding originally. Now that the idea no longer scared me, I would no doubt go through them again in the near future and throw out even more. It didn't matter to me that I wasn't a perfect Level One or Two, it didn't matter that I still had some stuff that was probably worthless to other people, what mattered was that for the first time ever, I controlled the stuff instead of the stuff controlling me.

Friends came to visit and oohed and aaahed at my parquetry floors and dishwasher. Adam showed up with a bottle of champagne and we drank it in the courtyard, sunning ourselves in the last of the day's rays and picking little bits of clover from between the pavers. Wendy came around and offered to help me drill holes for picture hooks in the walls.

'You've got to do something to mark it as your own, Corinne.' She grinned at me. 'It's not your house until you make a hole in it.'

It usually took months before anywhere new truly felt like my own and not the place of someone else with my stuff in it. Wendy was right, I needed to do something to make it mine. However, this was no mere rental and, as such, it needed a grand gesture. It needed a house-warming. I looked around. I could have a really big party here.

I wrote out the names of all the people I wanted to invite. Then I scrolled through my computer address book, just in case there was anyone I had forgotten. Katie's email address popped out. I had bumped into my childhood friend from Corryong in the city one day about a month ago. She still looked the same, with red hair and a big, carefree smile. It was so good to see her again. We'd swapped details and promised to keep in touch. Now seemed like the perfect time to do exactly that. I added her name to the list.

In total, I sent out twenty-five invitations. Twenty-five would be the capacity this house could hold before it started to feel like we were all trapped in a shipping container. I designed a little invitation, put together a group email and hit the send button.

As soon as the first RSVP came through I realised my mistake. I had not taken into consideration that most of my friends had partners. I hadn't invited twenty-five people, I'd invited fifty. I ran in circles around the few rooms of my home, counting on my fingers how many people I thought could fit in each. As long as everyone didn't arrive at the same time, and as long as twelve people didn't mind spending the entire party in the court-yard and another five were happy to limit themselves to sitting on my bed, we were probably going to be fine.

It hadn't occurred to me that throwing a big party might be stressful. I'd always imagined it would be a little bit like a 1950s movie and I'd be swanning around like Doris Day, making people martinis and belting out show tunes. Instead, I was running around a party supply store grabbing plastic cups, disposable ashtrays and industrial-strength stain remover. I flitted through the house cherry-picking anything I thought looked either dangerous or easily swallowed by a child or Adam. To my surprise, I effortlessly found room for all of the breakables in my wardrobe upstairs. The concept of 'spare space' was still new to me, and on the day of the party I lost half an hour of precious preparation time staring in wonder at my neatly arranged bedroom wardrobe.

Katie and her husband were amongst the first to arrive and I placed their bottles of wine in the ice-packed bath, poured them each a glass of champagne then grabbed them by the wrists and pulled them upstairs for a tour. I was, perhaps, a little over-eager.

'You can look in anything—anything!' I said, opening the bedroom door. 'All the drawers and cupboards are neat and tidy!' I dragged them back down to the kitchen. 'Look in here, there's just glasses! Just *glasses*!'

Adam planted his hands on my shoulders.

'Corinne, maybe you should calm down and have a gin and tonic. Or a Valium. Let me welcome the guests, okay? There's really no need to force people to look in your bathroom vanity.'

He was right. I hadn't seen Katie properly in years. It was probably best if I didn't behave as if I was still eight years old.

As more people turned up, I left Adam to shepherd them around. Back in the bad old days, I never would have allowed people to tramp around my place unaccompanied; they might have walked into the bedroom and discovered the forty tonnes of stuff that had been removed from the lounge and dumped on the bed, or they might have opened a cabinet door and been concussed by an avalanche of cassette tapes by Roxette and New Kids on the Block.

'*Mi casa, su casa!*' I yelled gaily as Adam took a couple up the stairs. He rolled his eyes at me.

However, as more and more people arrived, I started to worry. I was getting dangerously close to capacity and there were still more guests to come. A few people rang to cancel and I accepted their apologies with relief. If three or four more people turned up right now, I would have to walk outside and shove them in with my feet.

The party, which had started in the early afternoon, went until after midnight, and Katie was there right until the end. I was glad she'd stayed; with so many people in the house, I hadn't had a chance to talk to her properly. Now we were sitting on the lounge-room floor, reminiscing and laughing hysterically about the ridiculous things we had done as children. Although we'd both had far too much to drink already, Katie refilled our glasses with the last of the wine.

'Do you remember the time we were trying to be like the Famous Five? We chased that panel van down the street because we were convinced the guy who drove it was a kidnapper.' She was giggling helplessly.

'If he actually had been a kidnapper, why were we *following* him?' I was almost as floppy with laughter as she was and I was having trouble holding my glass still.

'Or that time we tried to record our own version of *The Man From Snowy River* and we had to give up because we kept giggling over the line "all the cracks had gathered to the fray"? Remember? We thought it meant a lot of bum cracks riding horses. It was the funniest thing in the world to us back then.'

'I think I've drunk enough to *still* think it's the funniest thing in the world.'

We kept telling old stories and laughing until our sides hurt.

Katie looked at me, grinning.

'I'm really glad we've got back in contact, Corinne.'

I grabbed her hand. 'Me too.'

I thought of the little girl I had been—back when I was that nervous, skinny kid who wouldn't let anyone borrow her pencils in case one of them went missing and the world ended. Now here I was in my own house, sitting on the floor surrounded by empty bottles and not even bothering to check if the parquetry had been scratched, if there were marks on the walls or if anything had been broken.

After Katie left, I sat on the couch and grinned. I was the kind of person who had friends and parties and a tidy house. I was the kind of person I'd always wanted to be.

Late the following afternoon, Adam came around to help with the cleaning up. There wasn't much to do; I'd finished most of it the night before in an effort to sober up. As we were fossicking in the courtyard for cigarette stubs, he pulled something out of a shrub and looked at me, concerned.

'Are you okay with this?'

He was holding up a broken champagne glass. I frowned.

'It's just a glass.'

He squealed.

'Oh my god! Can you imagine saying "it's just a glass" a year ago? I probably would have got a phone call from you in the middle of the night, crying about how that glass reminded you of some kid from high school, or your nanna's cat or something.'

I rolled my eyes. 'I wasn't *that* bad, Adam.'

'Do you remember the time you accidentally chipped the corner of a wooden pencil case you'd made in year nine?'

'Oh. Okay, maybe I was that bad.'

'You nearly threw yourself out the bedroom window!'

I laughed. 'Oh, shut up. And put that glass down before you cut yourself. I don't want the decking stained with your blood.'

He left that night and I sat down in my new study, staring out the little window to the alleyway behind. I hadn't checked my email in two days and was expecting a deluge of junk mail to delete. As the advertisements for dodgy electronics, even dodgier medications and the offers to 'make it last all night' scrolled down my screen, I noticed an email from Jordan. That was weird, I hadn't heard from him since I'd returned from Bali.

Hello Australian! You sent a message for another Jordan! Or do you want me to come to Australia?

I'd accidentally sent him an invite to my house-warming instead of sending it to a friend with the same name in Australia. I smiled at his broken English, still a hundred times better than my French.

So what is new? My friend has a boat in Bali and we are going for it in October. Why for you not making this cruise with us?

I looked around my study. Here were my books, all neatly in their shelves, here were my wardrobe doors, closing easily and storing the things I truly cherished. Here was the house that I had bought, the stuff that I loved, the memories that meant the most. There was nothing holding me back. I smiled and thought to myself, Why for not indeed?

Twenty-Two
Lessons in Letting Go

Here is a list of the things I learnt during the year it took me to de-hoard my life. It's certainly not a finite list; I'm still learning now. That's the great thing about getting to the bottom of all your junk: you get to the bottom of yourself at the same time. If you're a hoarder, maybe you'll find something here that will help.

On the other hand, if you're not sure whether you're a hoarder, here's a little test that might help: if someone gave you this book as a gift, *they were trying to tell you something.*

1 You don't need to travel to the Middle East, lose your best friend or discover an old man has died to find the motivation to start de-hoarding. (Frankly, I went a bit overboard.) But you do need to sit down and figure out why you are holding on to things in the first place. Is it fear? Regret? Guilt? Is it something else? Can you remedy these things? If not, is holding on to the object doing anything other than causing you more pain? Ask yourself questions, write about it, talk with friends. Once you've made sense of why you hoard, the letting go will be much easier.

2 Don't tackle the really painful stuff first, you'll only discourage yourself. Work up to it. You'll find you get tougher the longer you stick at it and, eventually, you'll build up the emotional equivalent of abs of steel. Once you've done that, then you can revisit the painful things without worrying that you'll end up sitting in a corner rocking back and forth.

3 This is not going to take a day or two like it does on TV—not if you want to do it properly and get to the bottom of why you hoard in the first place. Don't set yourself unrealistic goals about getting things done in record time. Instead, just promise yourself to keep going, steadily and regularly, until you reach your goal. Think of it as weight loss for your house.

4 Once you've made the decision to throw something out, throwing out similar things will be easy. Keep one item that reminds you of a particular time and place (your time machine) and get rid of the rest. You might still end up with a bag of clothing or knick-knacks but if you're anything like me, you had ten bags of the crap to start with, so you're miles ahead. Also, when there's only one bag left, revisiting it and throwing out more in the future won't seem like such a daunting task. That one bag may eventually whittle itself down to just a couple of things.

5 Brace yourself for this one: like an alcoholic, you will always be a hoarder. However, you can become a *reformed* hoarder. Keep an eye on yourself, watch that cupboards don't start filling up again. Keep a bag for charity on the go at all times. (I actually use an old clothes hamper.) Have a regular spot for it, maybe in the bottom of a wardrobe, or beside your desk. That way, whenever you happen upon something that you are ready to let go of, you can do it immediately. Too often we see things in drawers or cupboards and think to ourselves, 'Next time I do a clean-out, I'll throw that away.' The problem is, if you're saying that forty-five times a day, you're never going to remember all the things to ditch. So ditch them now. You'll be surprised how quickly your regular charity bag fills up. I probably do a run to the op shop once every three months and it feels good every time.

6 If it's really going to hurt to throw it out, then don't. Wait. Leave it in a high-traffic area of your house for a few days. I had an old bag that I had used when I was a teen-ager. The handles were broken beyond repair and I knew it had to go. Still, I felt bad about it. So I sat it on the floor of the kitchen and after three days of looking at what was essentially a mess of ripped-up nylon, I realised it was a ridiculous thing to put back in a cupboard. I carried it out to the bin, hugged it goodbye, then threw it out. It was a little bit sad, but then again, so is watching *Beaches*.

7 Pack away like with like. I've packed all my primary-school stuff in one box, high-school in another, university in another. All my tools are in one place, linen is in one cupboard, photo albums are on one bookshelf and so on. Also, all my balls of hair and fingernail-parings are stashed in a little purse and kept under my pillow. (I'm kidding, clearly.) Pack your things away in whatever theme you like, just ensure it makes sense to you. This will also make it easier if you start adding to those boxes in the future, as you'll be able to see if you're doubling up. Remember, you only need one thing from each time or place to be your time machine.

8 If, despite your best intentions, you come across something that really hurts, or conjures up a big painful memory that slams you in the side of the head, stop. Just stop. Breathe. Cry if you need to. Write about it. Call a friend. Watch a Will Ferrell movie. Then eat a lot of ice-cream and congratulate yourself on how far you've come. Don't revisit it again until those emotional abs of steel of yours are rock hard.

9 Don't throw out things in anger; you can't punish someone else by punishing yourself. Giving away a perfectly good bedside table won't make your ex wake in the night in a vale of tears, it'll just leave you with nowhere to put your alarm clock. Revisit it when you've calmed down. You'll probably let go of it in the end anyway, but at least you will have done it rationally.

10 That said, if you break up with someone, get rid of the bed linen immediately. I wish I had. I slept under the doona I had shared with Thomas for ages after we broke up. That's just creepy. And a bit gross.

11 You're going to find you have more money. I don't lose things now; I don't have to buy a new pair of scissors every time I need to cut something. My bills get paid on time because I know where I keep them. I don't have to leave the house to have dinner anymore, I actually enjoy being in my own home. *I'm* in control now, not the stuff.

12 If you can't get going on your own, get some friends to come around. People won't hate you for having a messy house, they'll love you. This is because they'll either see themselves in you and feel less alone in their plight, or they'll feel better about themselves because they're not in nearly the same dire pile of crap that you are. Either way, you're getting the help you need, and doing a community service at the same time.

13 Don't get discouraged. You're going to get a long way into this before anything looks any different. Just keep going. All of a sudden, after weeks and weeks of feeling like you've made no difference, you'll throw out one more thing and realise you can rearrange all your cupboards and move a whole mass of useful stuff into a new, cleared-out area. This will make you feel like a god. Build yourself a shrine, put on a toga, shave your head and make your family worship you.

14 Get a personal organiser when you're at your lowest, not when you're at your most motivated. They are there to help you when you get stuck.

15 Tell people you're clearing out your stuff. That way, the fear of being publicly shamed if you fail will keep you motivated.

16 Reward yourself. Throwing out all your old clothes will make you realise what a truly shabby wardrobe you actually have. Buy yourself something decent. Just one thing.

17 I said, just one thing.

18 With the above in mind, every time you buy a new something, throw out an old equivalent. Every time I buy a new article of clothing, I ditch something else. And if I have nothing that needs throwing out, I probably don't need anything new. Exceptions to this rule include special occasion clothes (weddings, fancy-dress parties, mountaineering), things that you actually need more than one of (such as underpants, socks, jumpers) or things that are missing (for example, you don't own any trousers; it happens). When you've got your wardrobe under control, you'll know exactly what you need and what you don't.

19 Make sure you put on a party CD. Don't play something miserable or something sentimental; you'll start looking at that old milk jug and reminiscing about all the good times you had together and then, the next thing you know, you'll be sitting on the floor sobbing over your possessions like they're real people and refusing to let them go. It's useful to keep reminding yourself that you are de-hoarding, not re-enacting a scene from *Sophie's Choice*. Treat the whole thing like a celebration; disco is good, anything from the eighties is better.

20 You don't have to throw out everything you've ever owned. I didn't and I have no intention of doing so. People who throw out everything and live without any reminders of their past are just as lost as the people who have thrown out nothing. We all have a story and we owe it to ourselves to honour that. I still have stuff that is useless to other people but means a lot to me. *Most people do.* Just throw out the duplicates, the stuff that is irrelevant and the stuff that makes you feel miserable or guilty or angry. Throw out the stuff that doesn't sing to you.

21 Don't let others bully you into tidying up *their* way. There are no rules. You can get rid of stuff in big chunks, do it one thing at a time, give it to charity, give it to friends, leave it on the footpath with a sign that says 'free to good home', do a naked dance in the middle of the street while throwing your stuff over your neighbour's fence or do a combination of all the above. It doesn't matter as long as the stuff goes and *you* feel like *you've* done it the right way. If it was as simple as just chucking everything out in one fell swoop, we all would have done it years ago. It's more complicated and more personal than that. Tell that to the next smartarse who makes a joke about your stuff. Either that, or collapse in front of them, wailing in grief and self-flagellating. They'll be so embarrassed they'll never bring it up again.

22 It's useful to find something that will remind you of where your hoarding started and display it as a reminder. For me, it's that ball of finger-knitting I made when I was eight years old. I found it not long ago when I was at my parents' house. I'd been going through a box in their spare room and when I pulled it out, I couldn't believe how small it was. I stared at it disbelievingly and thought to myself, '*This* is where it all started?' Obviously I'd allowed things to snowball. So now it sits in my study to remind me that everything is small to begin with. It's up to us to control how big we let it grow.

Good luck.

Acknowledgements

A big thankyou to everyone who helped me write this book, for all of your encouragement, cups of tea and especially for telling me your own hoarding stories, some which made me feel much better about myself. Thank you to Matthew Albert, Dana Bajjali from the UNHCR in Jordan, Ariane Rummery from the UNHCR in Australia, and all the refugees who shared their stories with me. Thank you to Maria Hofstra, Jordan and Fabian, Lucy Petry and her family. Thank you to Craig Ross, Lara Stockdale, Fahey Younger, Gerard McCullough, Don, Elizabeth and Wendy Grant, Nigel Cooper, Lissanne Oliver, Kellie Maltagliati, Paul Robinson, Annette Barlow, Angela Handley, Ali Lavau and the delightful Catherine Milne. And thank you to Adam Richard, who read over every word in this book and helped me back out of the forest on more than one occasion. In return, he wants everyone to know that, in this book, he is thinner than in real life.

About the Author

Corinne is an accomplished stand-up, MC, presenter, writer and broadcaster, and has performed both nationally and internationally. Best known for her work on *Rove Live* and *The Glasshouse*, she has also been seen in successful live shows everywhere from the Sydney Opera House to the Kalgoorlie Arts Centre. Her natural, down-to-earth charm and her quick wit have made her one of Australia's best-known, and most loved, performers.